Dennis Magner

The Standard Horse and Stock Book

A complete pictorial encyclopedia of practical reference for horse and stock owners

Dennis Magner

The Standard Horse and Stock Book
A complete pictorial encyclopedia of practical reference for horse and stock owners

ISBN/EAN: 9783337218362

Printed in Europe, USA, Canada, Australia, Japan

Cover: Foto ©Lupo / pixelio.de

More available books at **www.hansebooks.com**

AGRICULTURAL SERIES No. 1
JANUARY 2, 1894.

ISHED WEEKLY.
PRICE, $12.50 PER YEAR.

THE STANDARD

HORSE AND STOCK ..BOOK..

By PROF. D. MAGNER

Assisted in special departments by thirteen of America's leading Veterinary Surgeons and Inspectors.

Over Seventeen Hundred Illustrations.

PUBLISHED WEEKLY BY
THE WERNER COMPANY,
AKRON, OHIO.

Copyright, 1893, The Werner Company.

MAGNER'S STANDARD
HORSE AND STOCK BOOK

A Complete Pictorial Encyclopedia of Practical Reference
for Horse and Stock Owners,

COMPRISING

ALL SECRETS OF TAMING, CONTROLLING, AND EDUCATING UNBROKEN AND VICIOUS
HORSES, WITH THE DETAILS OF BREAKING UP ALL HABITS TO
WHICH HORSES ARE SUBJECT; THEIR ABUSES,
DISEASES, AND REMEDIES.

ALSO

FULL DESCRIPTIONS AND ILLUSTRATIONS

OF THE VARIOUS BREEDS OF CATTLE; SHEEP RAISING; SWINE AND THEIR DISEASES,
THE POULTRY INTEREST; THE DOG AND HIS AILMENTS, BEE CULTURE;
FRUIT CULTURE; GRAFTING; INSECTS INJURIOUS TO
FRUIT, ETC.; AND A PLEA FOR BIRDS.

Comprising Over 1200 Pages and 1756 Illustrations.

BY D. MAGNER,

AUTHOR OF THE NEW SYSTEM OF TAMING AND EDUCATING HORSES, INDORSED BY ROBERT BONNER, ESQ.,
AND ALL LEADING EXPERTS, AS THE BEST IN THE WORLD;

Assisted in Special Departments by JAS. HAMILL, D. V. S., Pres't Nat'l Vet. Med. Ass'n ; CHAS. A.
MEYER, D. V. S., Editor Veterinary Gazette, N. Y.; JOHN A. MCLAUGHLIN, D. V. S., Ex-Veterinary Inspector N. J. State Board of Health ; D. G. SUTHERLAND, Ex-Pres't Mich. State Vet.
Ass'n ; PAUL PAQUIN, A. M., V. S., Prof. of Vet. Science in State Ag. College, Columbia,
Mo.; T. BENT COTTON, M. D., V. S., Pres't O. St. Vet. Ass'n and Vice-Pres. Nat'l Med.
Vet. Ass'n ; Dr. B. C. MCBETH, Sec'y Mich. St. Vet. Ass'n. Hon. Mem. N. Y. St.
Ac. of Vet. Science ; J. A. DELL, V. S., Pres't Mich. St. Vet. Ass'n ; A. J.
CHANDLER, V. S., V.-Pres. Mich. St. Vet. Ass'n ; S. BRENTON, V. S.,
Ex-Pres't Mich. State Vet. Ass'n ; WM. JOPLING, V. S., Treas.
Mich. St. Vet. Ass'n ; A. I. ROOT, Author of "A B C of
Bee Culture;" JOHN A. ADAMS, Horticulturist.

CHICAGO:
THE WERNER COMPANY.
1893

Copyright 1887
by
D. MAGNER

Copyright 1893
by
THE WERNER COMPANY

Leading Veterinary Surgeons who assisted in preparing the Medical and Stock Departments of "The Standard Horse and Stock Book."

1 JAMES HAMILL, D. V. S.
2 T. BENT. COTTON, V. S.
3 PAUL PAQUIN, A. M. V. S.
4 A. J. CHANDLER, V. S.
5 JOHN A. MCLAUGHLIN, V. S.
6 CHAS. A. MEYER, V. S.
7 D. G. SUTHERLAND, V. S.
8 DR. B. C. MCBETH.
9 J. A. DELL, V. S.
10 S. BRENTON. V. S.

PREFACE.*

THERE are eleven million horses in the United States, and not one man in a million who knows how to educate them to the highest degree of usefulness. We say *educate*; for the horse is an animal of high and spirited organization, endowed by his Creator with capabilities and faculties which sufficiently resemble man's to come under the same general law of education and government. Primarily, the word educate means to *lead out* or *lead up*; and it is by the process of *leading out* and *leading up* a child's faculties that the child becomes a useful man, and it is by a like process that a colt becomes a useful horse. Now, teachers, like poets, are born, not made. Only a few are gifted to see into and through any form of highly organized life, discern its capacities, note the interior tendencies which produce habits, and discover the method of developing the innate forces until they reach their noblest expression, and then apply the true and sufficient guidance and government. The few who have this gift are teachers indeed, and, next to the mothers of the world, deserve the world's applause as foremost among its benefactors.

Next to child training and government comes horse training and government; and which is the least understood, it were

---

*This preface was written by a gentleman well known in the world of letters, and especially famous, not only as a lover of fine horses, but as a high authority on all matters concerning them. Learning that I had in preparation a new work, he volunteered to write the preface, which is here given as a concise introduction to the author's own labors, with a high appreciation of the compliment paid him by the distinguished writer, in the personal allusion, the publication of which demands no apology when its high source is considered.

hard to say. Boys and colts, so much alike in friskiness and stubbornness, both are misunderstood and abused in equal ratio. The boys are shaken and whipped, and the colts are yanked, kicked, and pounded. That high-spirited or slow-witted boys become good men, and high-spirited or dull colts make serviceable horses, I conceive is due to the grace of God more than to man's agency,—that fine grace, I mean, spread abroad through and existing in all His creatures, which operates in regenerating continually, making the good better, and preventing those whose circumstances forbid their becoming good from becoming absolutely bad.

The author of this book is known to me as one of the gifted ones of the earth, because he is gifted to discern the nature of animals, and educate them for man's service. The possession of this gift suggested his mission, and well has he followed it, and by it been educated himself to a degree rarely, if ever, attained by man before. I doubt if there be on the globe his equal in knowledge as to the best method of training horses. Through this volume he seeks to give the public the benefit of his experience. I bespeak for it the careful perusal of the curious, and of those especially whose judgment and heart alike prompt them to seek for and promulgate knowledge, which, being popularized, would make the people more humane and horses more serviceable.

W. H. H. M.

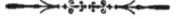

LAW OF COPYRIGHTS.

THE exclusive benefits of copyrights extend to twenty-eight years, then renewable for fourteen years; if the author is dead, to the heirs, by re-recording, and advertising the re-record for four weeks in any newspaper in the United States.

The forfeiture of all the books, and a penalty of fifty cents on each sheet (sixteen pages) of the work, half to the United States, and half to the author, is the penalty for publishing or importing any work without the written consent of the author; and the printer is equally liable with the publisher.

Entries must be sent to the Librarian of Congress at Washington, D. C. The laws are found in Vol. IV. of the United States Statutes, pages 436–439.

This Work, with " Facts for Horse Owners," from which the part on the horse is taken, is protected by three separate Copyrights, covering, first, its Title; second, its Literary Composition; and third, its Engravings.

There are also three patents covering important methods of subjection and treatment given in this book. First, a simple means of subjection by which any horse, however vicious, balky, or unmanageable, can be put in harness, subdued, and driven gently without danger of accident. Second, a method by which headstrong, lunging, runaway horses can be controlled directly, and so subdued by the pressure of the reins upon the nerve centers, that he will soon submit to the ordinary restraint of the bit. Third, a method of preventing and curing contraction and quarter-crack—an absolute cure for quarter-crack, with freedom to drive on any road as desired, without causing the hoof to split back as it grows—guaranteed a means of perfect cure. Fourth (patent pending), a method by which most horses pulling or lugging on the bit, will drive safely and easily to a pleasant and easy restraint of the reins.

Purchasers of this Work or " Facts for Horse Owners " from the author or his agents, will be entitled to the use of either or all of these patents (for personal use only), without extra charge; all others using them will be subject to legal proceedings.

Veterinary Surgeons.

TWENTY-FIVE years ago, there were but very few veterinary surgeons in the country, and these were located exclusively in the larger cities; and there were no veterinary schools for their instruction. During recent years, the better informed classes of the community have become so awakened to the importance of treating the diseases of domestic animals **intelligently,** in accordance with **scientific principles,** that there have been established quite a number of well-conducted veterinary colleges in this country and Canada; and in consequence there are now to be found, in most of the larger towns in all the States, **intelligent, well-trained, and competent men,** who have graduated from such colleges.

Now, I am in a position to know that the training in these schools is designed to be very thorough, and that those at their head are **well qualified for their positions;** and a certificate of graduation from any of these colleges should be sufficient to give **entire confidence** in the competency of the person holding it, and entitle him to the encouragement of stock owners. It cannot be denied that veterinary surgeons trained in this way are, as a class, among the most useful and hard-working men in any of the professions, and should be **respected and encouraged accordingly.**

So, if you have a horse or other animal that has been injured or become sick, especially if a valuable animal, it is by all means advisable to **call in a veterinary surgeon,** provided there be one within reach; and this should be done at once, without the hazard of delay. No matter how plain the instructions given in this book may seem, the **safest and wisest course** will be to employ such a man, if available. Even though a man is not a regular graduate, if he has the reputation of being successful in practice, it will be best to employ him.

In this, as in other professions, there are men who have such **natural ability** as to become very successful in practice. If I had a horse taken sick, even though I knew just what to do, I should be induced to call in the aid of a veterinary surgeon, if there was one obtainable. **So do not give the cold shoulder to the veterinary** who may come with proper qualifications to locate in your neighborhood, but extend to him the encouragement of your early **and cordial support.**

TABLE OF CONTENTS.

PART FIRST.

CHAPTER I.
Preliminary Explanations.
The Instincts of Lower Animals—Their Remarkable Powers—Adaptation of Domestic Animals to Special Wants of Man—Principles of Treatment—Necessary Qualifications for Success in Controlling Vicious Horses. . 25

CHAPTER II.
Principles and Secrets of the Art of Taming and Educating Horses.
Special Points of Importance—The War Bridle—Principles of its Application—The "W," or Breaking Bit—Training the Mouth—Four-ring, or Upper Jaw Bit—Half-moon Bit—Spoon Bit—Patent Bridle—Foot Strap—Patent Breaking Rig. 52

CHAPTER III.
Colt Training.
How to Make the Colt Gentle—Teaching to be Ridden, Handled, and to Follow—Various Methods—Making a Wild Colt Follow Instantly—How to Make any Sullen Colt Lead—Teaching a Colt or Horse to Follow with the Whip—Making the Colt Fearless of Objects and Sounds—Driving any Colt in Harness without Breeching—Training the Mouth, Biting, etc. . 106

CHAPTER IV.
Fear.
Susceptibility to Fear—How to Prevent and Overcome It—Illustrative Cases—Fear of Rattle of Wagon—Jumping out of Shafts—Top Carriage—Objects Exciting Fear while Riding or Driving—A Robe—Umbrella or Parasol—Sound of a Gun—Hogs and Dogs—Railroad Cars—Insanity. . . . 130

CHAPTER V.
Kicking.
Causes of Kicking—How to Prevent and Overcome It—Driving any Kicker without Breeching—Switching Kickers—Kickers in Stall—While Harnessing—Nervous Kickers—Kicking while Grooming—Runaway Kickers. . . 148

CHAPTER VI.
Running Away.

Runaway Kickers—Different Methods of Controlling the Mouth—How to Hold any Horse—Lugging, or Pulling upon One Rein—Making a Horse Back. 183

CHAPTER VII.
Balking.

Preventing the Habit—Different Methods of Starting the Balker—How to Break up the Habit—Different Tricks Used—Will not Stand when Getting in or out of a Wagon—Double Balking—An Easy Method of Breaking a Double Balker. 193

CHAPTER VIII.
Bad to Shoe.

Taking up the Colt's Foot—Easy Method of Controlling Colts—Confirmed in the Habit—Simple Method of Making a Horse Stand to be Shod—The Control of Very Difficult Cases—Leaning Over. 209

CHAPTER IX.
Halter-Pulling.

How to Prevent any Colt or Horse from Halter-pulling—How to Break any Horse of the Habit—Running Back in the Stall when Unhitched—Standing Without Being Hitched—Hitching any Horse so that he will not Pull after Two or Three Minutes. 222

CHAPTER X.
Stallions.

Care in their Management—Treatment for Headstrong Stallions—Treatment for Very Vicious Stallions—How to Subdue and Control any Stallion so that he can be Called away from a Mare in a few Minutes—Special Tests Illustrating the Ease with which this can be Done. 232

CHAPTER XI.
Checking and Blinders.

Cruelty of Checking—The Foolishness of the Practice—Injurious to the Horse—Covering the Eyes—A Bad, Senseless Custom. 246

CHAPTER XII.
The Mule.

His Subjection and Management. 263

CHAPTER XIII.
Miscellaneous Habits.

Cribbing—Wind-sucking—Putting the Tongue out of the Mouth—Pawing in Stall—Kicking in Stall—Getting Cast in Stall—Jumping over Fences—Tender-bitted—Kicking Cows—To Lead a Cow Easily. . . . 266

CHAPTER XIV.
Teaching Tricks.

To Follow by the Whip—To Throw Boys—To Drive without Reins—To Tell the Age, etc., etc. 275

CHAPTER XV.
Equestrianism.
Horseback Riding—Its Beneficial Effects upon the Health—Teaching to Ride—Position in the Saddle—A Model Riding Horse, etc. 286

CHAPTER XVI.
Breeding.
Principles of Breeding—Methods Adopted in Foreign Countries, etc. . 296

CHAPTER XVII.
Stabling.
Construction of Stable—Air and Light—Form of Manger. . 301

CHAPTER XVIII.
Feeding and Watering.
Cooked Food—Mr. Bonner's System. 307

CHAPTER XIX.
How to Tell the Age Accurately.
Caries of the Teeth—Treatment. 313

CHAPTER XX.
Shoeing.
Principles of Shoeing—Tips and Thin Shoes—Contraction—A Reliable Method of Preventing and Curing Contraction—Old Methods of Treating it—Quarter-crack—Simple Method of Curing Any Case—Crack, or Fissure of Toe—Corns—Causes, and Practical Method of Curing—Weak Heels—Their Management—Interfering—Clicking, or Overreaching — Stumbling — Shoeing Sore or Foundered Horses—Causes of Injury in Shoeing. 329

DISEASES AND THEIR TREATMENT.

CHAPTER XXI.
The Circulation—General Plan of the Circulatory System—Derangements of that System the Cause of Disease—Importance of Ventilation. . . . 401

CHAPTER XXII.
Anchylosis—Caries—Necrosis — Exostosis, or Bony Enlargement — Splints — Spavins—Ring-bone—Side-bone, or False Ring-bone—Curb—Bog Spavins and Thorough-pins—Capped Hock—Wind-galls—Navicular-joint Lameness—Founder—Chronic Founder—Peditis. 411

CHAPTER XXIII.
SEC. 1. Catarrh—Laryngitis—Distemper—Glanders and Farcy—Chronic Cough—Heaves, or Broken Wind—Roaring—Bronchocele—Nasal Gleet—Influenza, Epizootic, or Catarrhal Fever—Pink-eye—Congestion of the Lungs—Pleurisy—Pneumonia—Hydrothorax—Typhoid Pneumonia—Bronchitis. . 453

x   CONTENTS.

SEC. 2. Colic—Flatulent Colic—Inflammation of the Bowels—Superpurgation
—Diarrhea—Constipation—Worms—Bots—Inflammation of the Kidneys—
Profuse Staling—Inflammation of the Bladder—Retention of Urine—Bloody
Urine—Inflammation of the Brain—Vertigo—Sun-stroke. 493

SEC. 3. Spinal Meningitis — Paralysis — Lock-jaw—Stringhalt—Thumps—Lymphangitis—Weed—Monday Morning Leg—Peritonitis—Indigestion—Acidity
of the Stomach—Acute Indigestion. 524

CHAPTER XXIV.

SEC. 1. The Foot—Pricking in Shoeing—Stepping on Nails, Glass, etc.—Foot
Lameness—Seedy Toe—Graveling—Bruise of the Sole—Treads, or Calks—
Overreach—Quittor—Thrush—Canker. 536

SEC. 2. Sprains, Bruises, etc.—Sprain of the Back Tendons—Breaking Down
—Sprain of the Fetlock—Shoulder Lameness—Sweeney—Hip Lameness—
Knuckling Over—Broken Knees, or Open Joint—Fractures—Dislocation of
Patella—Stifle-joint Lameness. 548

SEC. 3. Cuts or Wounds—Sore Mouth—Fistula of the Withers—Poll-evil—
Diseases of the Eye—Dropsy—Swelled Legs. 568

SEC. 4. Diseases of the Skin—Surfeit—Nettle Rash, Hives, etc.—Mange—Hen
Lice—Ring-worm—Scratches—Grease—Tumors— Sallenders — Saddle and
Collar Galls—Tenotomy—Castration—Parturition—Counter-irritants — Fomentations—Poultices—The Pulse—Giving Balls—Physicking—Bleeding—
Setons—The Rowel — Tracheotomy—Embrocations—Liniments—Rheumatism, Acute and Chronic—Warts. 592

PART SECOND.

DAIRYING.

CHAPTER I.
Breeds of Cattle.

Importance of the Dairying Interest—Desirable Points in a Cow—The Milk Escutcheon—The Several Varieties of Cattle — Short-horns—Long-horns—
Polled Cattle. 643

CHAPTER II.
Feeding Cows.

Influence of Feeding on the Production of Milk—Importance of Care in Selection of Food—Value of Air and Exercise—Best Kinds of Food—Artificial
Feeding—Regulation of Food. 652

CHAPTER III.
Milking—Raising Calves.

Milking To-day and in the Past—Stripping—Sore Teats—Importance of Cleanliness in Milking—Calving—Feed and Treatment before and during Calving
—Rearing of Calves—Anti-sucking Devices. 659

CHAPTER IV.
Hay-Making.
Hay to be as Nearly like Green Grass as Possible—Time to Cut Hay—Analysis of Clover Hay—Mowing-machines—Hay-makers—Horse-rakes—Hay-loaders—Drainage—Dairy Barns. 668

CHAPTER V.
Milk.
Physiology of Milk—Milk Secretion—Anatomy of the Udder—Composition of Milk—Cleanliness and Ventilation in Milk Houses—Disease Propagated through Milk. 676

CHAPTER VI.
Butter-Making.
Fat Globules—Cream-raising—Deep and Shallow Setting—Milk Tanks and Coolers—Milk Aerators—Strainers—Weighing-cans—Various Devices and Apparatus. 686

CHAPTER VII.
Butter-Making, Continued.
Churning—The Old and the New Way—Various Styles of Churn—Working Butter—Cleanliness—Salting—Butter-working Machines—Marketing Butter—Tubs and Jars. 697

CHAPTER VIII.
Cheese-Making.
Milk Vats—Refrigerating Vats—Self-heating Vats—Curd-mills and Curd-drainers—Curd-knives and Curd-breakers—Cheese-presses—Upright and Gang Presses—Cheese-hoops—Cheese-factories. 706

CHAPTER IX.
City Milk Delivery.
Cooling Milk for Transportation—Different Patterns of Milk-cans—Model Delivery Wagon—Depot Refrigerator—Koumiss—Its Value—Formulas for its Manufacture. 716

DISEASES OF CATTLE.

CHAPTER X.
Conditions of Health.
Prevention—Nursing—Proper Care—Alimentary Canal of Horse and Ox—Temperament of Cattle—Susceptibility to Diseases of the Blood—Non-susceptibility to Nervous Diseases—Administering Medicine—Doses—Difference in Action of Medicine in Cattle and Horses—Importance of Familiarity with the Appearance of Cattle in Health—Normal Pulse, Respiration, and Temperature. 721

CHAPTER XI.
Contagious Blood Diseases.
Pleuro-pneumonia — Rinderpest —Anthrax, Charbon, Bloody Murrain—Gloss

Anthrax, or Black Tongue—Black Leg—Splenetic Apoplexy—Epizootic Aphtha, or Foot and Mouth Disease—Cow-pox, or Variola Vaccini. . . 726

CHAPTER XII.
Non-Contagious Blood Diseases.
Plethora—Anæmia—Purpura Hæmorrhagica—Rheumatism—Uræmia—Hæmaturia, or Red-water—Septicæmia and Pyæmia. 741

CHAPTER XIII.
Diseases of Respiratory Organs.
Location of the Inflammatory Process—Auscultation and Percussion—Catarrh, Colds—Malignant Catarrh—Laryngitis, or Sore Throat—Malignant Sore Throat—Tracheotomy—Bronchitis—Pneumonia—Abscess of the Lungs—Pleurisy—Tapping of the Chest—Sporadic Pleuro-pneumonia—Asthma, or Emphysema. 752

CHAPTER XIV.
Diseases of Digestive Organs.
Drenching—Injuries of the Mouth—Inflammation of Mouth and Tongue—Stomach of Ruminants—Intestines of Ox—Lymphatics—Hoven—Probang and Gags—Puncturing the Rumen—Impacted Rumen, or Maw-bound—Rumenotomy—Obstruction of the Gullet—Impaction of Omasum. . . . 768

CHAPTER XV.
Diseases of Digestive Organs, Continued.
Dyspepsia—Rickets—Fragility of Bones—Diarrhea—Dysentery — Enteritis—Peritonitis—Abdominal Hernia—Strangulation of Intestines—Casting an Ox—German Method. 782

CHAPTER XVI.
Diseases of Urinary Organs.
Urinary Apparatus of Ox—Diabetes—Retention of Urine—Operation for Removing Urine—Incontinence of Urine—Albuminuria — Hæmaturia, or Bloody Urine—Sthenic Hæmaturia—Inflammation of the Kidneys—Inflammation of the Bladder—Gravel—Protrusion and Inversion of the Bladder. 792

CHAPTER XVII.
Nerve, Skin, and Eye Diseases.
Apoplexy—Epilepsy—Inflammation of the Brain—Nervous Debility in Parturition—Tetanus, or Lock-jaw—Eczema—Herpes—Foul in the Foot—Foreign Substances in the Eye—Ophthalmia. 801

CHAPTER XVIII.
Parasitic Diseases.
External Parasites—Gad-fly—Lice—Mange—Ring-worm—Internal Parasites—Hoose, or Verminal Bronchitis—Measles—Tape-worm. 808

CHAPTER XIX.
Parturition.
Period of Gestation—Signs of Parturition—Natural Parturition—Expulsion of Placenta—Unnatural Presentations of Various kinds—Retained After-birth. 817

CONTENTS. xiii

CHAPTER XX.
Parturient Diseases.

Flooding—Inversion of Uterus—Dr. Meyer's Treatment—Original and Successful Treatment by Dr. McBeth—Inflammation of the Uterus—Puerperal Fever—Parturient Apoplexy, or Milk Fever. 825

CHAPTER XXI.
Parturient Diseases, Continued.

Leucorrhea, or Whites—Abortion—Importance of Isolation—Hernia of the Uterus—Sore Teats—Gonorrhea—Mammitis, or Inflammation of the Udder—Treatment of Calves—Care at Birth—Their Ailments. 835

CHAPTER XXII.
Miscellaneous.

Teeth of Cattle—Study of Dentition—Unreliability of Determining Age by Horns—Teeth of Different Ages—Methods of Throwing and Securing the Ox—Throwing by a Single Rope—Rueff's Method—Securing the Ox in a Standing Position—Securing Hind Leg—Ox Travis—Nose-clamps—Nose-ring—Alsace Nose-ring and Headstall—Vigan's Apparatus—Devices to Prevent Hooking and Running—Yoke for Ox. 844

CHAPTER XXIII.
Local Injuries, Dislocations, and Wounds.

Injury of Stifle Joint—Dislocation of Patella—Kinds and Treatment of Wounds—Sutures, Needles, Syringes, and Bandages—Inflammatory Action and Fever—Cleanliness, Ventilation, and Disinfection—Forms of Contagious Matter—Disinfecting Agents—Chloride of Lime—Carbolic Acid—Sulphate of Iron—Sulphate of Zinc—Formulas for Disinfectants in Solid and Liquid Forms—Fumigation—Sulphur—Chlorine Gas. 855

SHEEP.

CHAPTER XXIV.
Breeds of Sheep.

Sheep in Ancient Times—Mutton a Modern Product—Statistics of Sheep-raising in the United States—Breeds of Sheep—Long-wooled Sheep—Short-wooled Sheep—Breeds of Sheep in Asia, Europe, and America—Wild Sheep. .863

CHAPTER XXV.
Care and Management.

Pasturage—Adaptation of Different Soils—Foods in Short Pasturage—Dry and Clean Pastures Essential—Treatment of Ewes During Gestation—Treatment and Feeding of Lambs—Docking and Castration—Lamb-creep—Weaning time—Selection of Rams and Ewes for Breeding—Dipping for Ticks—Washing and Shearing—Care and Feeding in Winter—Comparative Nutritive Value of Foods. 881

CHAPTER XXVI.
Diseases of Respiratory, Digestive, and Urinary Organs.
Structure of the Sheep—The Teeth—Causes of Disease—Catarrh—Bronchitis—Pneumonia—Pleurisy—Constipation—Diarrhea—Dysentery—Hoven—Inflammation of the Bladder—Retention of Urine—Sediment in Urinary Canal—Stone in the Bladder. 891

CHAPTER XXVII.
Blood, Nerve, Enzootic, and Epizootic Diseases.
"Pining"—Dropsy—Lock-jaw—Vertigo—Parturient Paraplegia—Eczema—Ecthyma—Psoriasis—Solary Ecthyma—Influenza—Red Water—Rot Dropsy—Foot-rot—Foot and Mouth Disease—Small Pox—Anthrax, or Quarter Ill—Tuberculosis—Rabies. 899

CHAPTER XXVIII.
Parasitic Diseases.
Revolution Wrought by the Microscope—Sheep-bots, or Grubs in the Head—The Fluke Disease, or Liver Rot—Different Varieties of Fluke—Vermicular Bronchitis—Turnsick, Sturdy, or Gid. 909

CHAPTER XXIX.
Parasitic Diseases, Continued.
The Tape-worm—Its Existence in the Intestines—Mange or Itch—Various Species of Acari—Dog-tick—Fodder-louse—Body-louse—Head-louse—Sheep-louse Sheep-tick—Sheep-bug—Man-eating Fly—Tsetse Fly. 919

CHAPTER XXX.
Lambing and Attendant Diseases.
Parturient Fever—Parturient Paralysis—Garget—Castration—Rheumatism—Cancer of the Foot—Docking—Fractures—Sprains—Feeling the Pulse. . 927

SWINE.
CHAPTER XXXI.
Anthrax and Cholera.
Diseases of Swine Largely Due to Improper Food and Management—Administering Medicines to Hogs—Charbon, Anthrax, or Hog Cholera—Nature of Anthrax Diseases—Gangrenous Erysipelas—Malignant or Gangrenous Angina—Apoplectic Anthrax—Preventive Measures. 933

CHAPTER XXXII.
Anthrax and Cholera, Continued.
So-called "Hog Cholera"—What the Term Implies—Contagious Pleuro-enteritis—Erysipelatous Form—Malignant Sore Throat—Various Remedies—Attributed to Contagion—Judicious Rules for Treatment. 944

CHAPTER XXXIII.
Catarrhal Diseases, etc.
Malignant Epizootic Catarrh—Apoplexy—"Snuffles"—Constipation—Diarrhea—Diphtheria—Epilepsy—Inflammation of the Lungs—Abscess—Anæmia—Piles. 954

CHAPTER XXXIV.
Parasites of Swine.
Kidney-worms—Hog-lice—Mange, or Scab—Measles in Pork—Trichinosis—The Strongylus—The Ascaris—Symptoms of Worms. . . . 970

POULTRY.

CHAPTER XXXV.
Breeds and Breeding.
Houdans—Crevecœurs—Cochins—Plymouth Rocks—Polish Fowls—Brahmas—Silkies—Frizzled Fowls—Rumpless Bantams—East India Fowls—Aseels—Sebright and Pekin Bantams—Sebastopol Geese—Nile Geese—Black-beaked Turkey—Ducks. 983

CHAPTER XXXVI.
Food, Feeding, and Marketing.
Proper Food for Fowls—Fattening for Market—Killing—Preserving and Packing Eggs—Proper Kinds of Food. 999

CHAPTER XXXVII.
Poultry Architecture.
General Directions—Portable Poultry Houses—Shelters—"Warm Mother"—"Cold Mother"—Coops—Improved Poultry Homes. . . . 1003

CHAPTER XXXVIII.
Eggs and Incubation.
Generation of the Egg—Physiology of Incubation—Natural Incubation—Convenient Hens' Nests—Egg-protector—Fertility and Egg-testers. 1008

CHAPTER XXXIX.
Artificial Incubation.
Artificial Incubators in Ancient Times—Progress in Invention of Incubating Machines—The Graves Incubator—Halsted's Automatic Incubator—The Boyle Incubator—Tomlinson's Automatic Incubator—Thermostatic Incubator—Hearson's Regulator. 1012

CHAPTER XL.
Diseases of Poultry.
Apoplexy—Bronchitis—Bumble-foot—Catarrh—Cholera—Consumption—Cramps—Crop-bound—Debility—Diarrhea—Diphtheria—Egg-bound—Feather-eating—Frost-bite—Gapes—Vertigo—Swelled Legs—Indigestion—Leg-weakness—Lice—Liver Disease—Pip—Roup—White-comb—Worms in Ducks—Caponizing Fowls. 1020

THE DOG.

CHAPTER XLI.
Races of Dogs.
The Dog's Close Relation to Man—His Intelligence—His Origin—Kinship of the Wolf, Hyena, Jackal, and Fox to the Dog—The Newfoundland Dog—

xvi   *CONTENTS.*

Tales of the Newfoundland—The St. Bernard—His Wonderful History
and Characteristics—Interesting Incidents.   1031

CHAPTER XLII.
Races of Dogs, Continued.
The Shepherd Dog—Incidents Illustrating his Sagacity—The Esquimau Dog—
The Danish Dog—The Bull-dog—The Brutality of Dog-fighting—The Greyhound—The Blood-hound—Illustrations of his Intelligence—The Terrier
—The Setter—The Dachshund—Pet Dogs.   1041

CHAPTER XLIII.
Diseases of Dogs.
Structure of the Dog—Distemper—Diarrhea and Dysentery—Constipation—Inflammation of the Bowels—Throat and Lung Diseases—Goitre—Hydrophobia — Parasites — The Round-worm — Giant Strongle—Tape-worm—Blood-sucker — Bird-louse — Ear-louse — Cat-flea—Dog-flea—Remedies for
Worms and Mange.   1053

BEE-CULTURE.
CHAPTER XLIV.

Importance of Bee-keeping as an Industry —Effect of Modern Progress in Bee-culture—Description of Bees—Process of Making Honey—Internal Economy of the Hive—Swarming—How to Manage and Prevent Swarming—Various Inventions Therefor—Artificial Swarming—Various Kinds of Hives—Bee Pasturage—Preparing Honey for Market—Liquid Honey—Honey Extractor—Comb Honey—Its Preparation—Root's Improvement on the Longstroth Hive—Guarding against Robbery of Hives—Preparing Bees for Winter—Proper Methods of Storing Honey.   1065

FRUIT CULTURE.
CHAPTER XLV.

Importance of the Culture of Fruit—Transplanting, Pruning, and Management
—Selection of Stock—Budding—Layering—Layering by Elevation—Approach-grafting—Cleft-grafting—Insects Injurious to Fruits—Remedies for
Them—General Hints for Protection of Fruits.   1087

PLEA FOR THE BIRDS.
CHAPTER XLVI.

The Usefulness as well as Delightfulness of Birds—The Benefit they Confer in
Destroying Insects—Eloquent Tribute of Rev. Henry Ward Beecher—Chiffchaff—Yellow Wren—Golden-crested Wren—Fire-crested Warbler—African
Beef-eater—Blue-bird— Pigmy Piculet—Rose-colored Pastor—Short-tailed
Ant Thrush—European Goat-sucker.   1107

INTRODUCTION.

For Special Reasons of Interest to the Reader, What is Written Here Should be Read First, and with Care.

PRIOR to 1860, when I was first betrayed into giving some special exhibitions in the art of taming horses, there was but very little known on the subject, and what was known could not be regarded as more than the merest empiricism. Indeed, I had been under the impression myself at that time, that there was some great secret, giftedness, scent, or medicines by which vicious horses could be controlled and changed in character. This impression had misled me greatly; and it was only by long-continued observation and practice that I was finally able, little by little, to grasp the subject in its true aspect, and learn the real principles of subduing and controlling vicious horses in a practically reliable manner.

The drift of my efforts and experiments which enabled me to do this, extended over many years, and during the first decade were necessarily but little more than a series of crude experiments, success being constantly alternated with more or less failure; and, in fact, I was deeply interested in the study, and was far from exhausting it, when I left the road at the expiration of over nineteen years of the most exacting experience before the public, and extending to all the older-settled States of the country. But every failure, when made, had been only the means of suggesting new points, revealing to me new and more correct insight into the study, thereby carrying me forward, and enabling me finally to accomplish results in the

SUBJECTION OF SPECIALLY VICIOUS HORSES,

which were not only a source of constant interest and surprise to myself, but of astonishment to the best horsemen in the country and the world, because of reducing the principles of controlling and educating horses to the basis of an exact science, and not only revolutionizing all previous ideas of the control and management of horses, but saving fully eighteen-twentieths of the time usually required in their training, as well as making it entirely safe and simple to do. The power to change, as if by magic, the character of a horse that had perhaps defied all previous effort to be brought under restraint, and proved in consequence to be practically worthless, frequently in the short period of less than an hour, could not but be accepted as a startling innovation to them, but, if possible, of more interest from the fact that these results were brought about by clear, well-defined principles of treatment, so plain, simple, and practical as to be easily understood and applied, and within the ability of any ordinary person to master and use.

These principles I was compelled to teach as a secret, for which I charged a fee of from five to ten dollars; which instructions were necessarily limited to a few hours, and to a few representative citizens in each neighborhood that I visited; and though I published a small work, which was included in the instructions, it was of necessity so written as not to impart these secrets, and would give no idea whatever of my methods and principles of treatment to persons who had not attended my lectures.

Though possessed, when young, of a remarkably strong constitution, the constant struggle and excitement forced upon me in so difficult a field for so many years, gradually undermined and impaired my health, until, in the early winter of 1878, I finally broke down so seriously as to be compelled to leave the road.

I now concluded to carry out at my leisure the purpose which had for some time been developing in my mind,—that of writing out the full details of my system, including such knowledge as I believed to be most valuable to horse owners, and that would bring it within the reach of people generally. I at first intended to make a work of only about three hundred pages, which would embody merely the simple outlines I gave to classes, with some additions to the treatment for sickness and lameness which I had already given in my old book. But after writing it up and preparing the illustrations I supposed necessary, I could see so much that should be added, that I was induced to re-write the whole matter, bringing it up to about six hundred pages, with about three hundred and fifty illustrations. When this was completed, I again found it necessary to make still more additions, until it grew upon my hands to the present size and number of illustrations of my regular book on this subject. With the enlargement of the work grew also upon me the desire to make the departments of **Shoeing, Sickness, and Lameness** equally satisfactory. With this object I made a special effort to secure the best veterinary skill I could command; but in this I entirely failed, until fortunate in arresting the attention of DR. JAMES HAMILL, D. V. S., of New York City, formerly Professor of Pathological Shoeing in the Columbia Veterinary College, whom I found to have attended my lectures in that city in the winter of 1872, and who exhibited the kindest interest in my efforts, not only volunteering all the aid in his power to give, but securing for me the aid of two of his colleagues, DR. CHAS. A. MEYER, N. Y. City, and DR. JOHN A. MC LAUGHLIN, then of Jersey City, N. J., now of Providence, R. I., both of whom occupied high positions in the profession. DR. HAMILL gave me every aid in his power, not only in preparing the chapter on Shoeing, for which he was specially qualified, but in other departments, and in addition, placed the use of his fine library freely at my disposal.

The better to facilitate my work, I had these gentlemen dictate to me the outlines of treatment required, in the simplest language possible, with permission to make any changes I desired. It is but just, also, to them, to explain that the dictations by them were in all cases made without premeditation, the point in view being to give me the facts most clearly and in the fewest words. This was the more difficult for them from the fact that they were limited to my ability to take notes, as, on account of the peculiarly sensitive condition of my health, I could endure but very brief conversation, and but thirty or forty minutes' writing at one time:

I was also specially indebted to PROF. E. A. MC LELLAN, of Bridgeport, Conn., who was at the time Lecturer on Shoeing and Diseases of the Foot in Columbia Veterinary College, who gave me much valuable aid in that department. DR. B. C. MC BETH, of Battle Creek, Mich., also rendered me very important assistance.

After five large editions of the book had been published, and meeting with the greatest favor, it was strongly urged upon me by a leading book publisher, to add a STOCK DEPARTMENT that would in general character correspond with the rest of the work as it then stood. In support of his assertion, he stated that there was not a single really practical or reliable work published on the subject, and that if I would make such a book, I would not only be sure of a large sale, but confer a substantial benefit upon the farming community.

There had also been from the first repeated and urgent inquiries by my agents for such an additional feature, it being given as a reason that while farmers were greatly interested in horses, and needed the instructions given, they strongly desired also the additional departments suggested.

Influenced by these considerations, I was led to consider the matter seriously. But I found there was no single professional man in the country, so far as I knew, who could write up all the departments of such a work in the practical manner I required, as men even in the very first ranks of the profession are only proficient in certain departments, necessarily depending upon the aid of standard authorities. Then, there was no one man in the country whose time could be made available for the purpose, even at a high compensation.

In this emergency, and advised by veterinary friends, I determined upon the following plan, as that giving promise of the best and most satisfactory results: First, to obtain all the standard veterinary authorities in the English and European languages, especially those in German and French, embodying the highest and most reliable authorities on the subjects treated ; next, the employing of thoroughly trained scholars capable of translating and collecting the requisite facts from such authorities, and under my special directions write them out in the plainest language for the treatment of each disease ; and the matter so prepared, on each subject, to be submitted to one or more experts for each department, with instructions to make such changes and additions as in their judgment would be advisable to render the matter of the best practical reference. To do this work I employed three of the best scholars to be obtained in the country, one of whom was a regular graduate of one of our leading medical colleges. This work required of itself nearly a year's time.

In the meantime I consulted special friends in the veterinary profession to learn who were the best expert practitioners to make the revisions and corrections I required, and was so fortunate as to secure the aid of the gentlemen whose names are here given, and who co-operated with me in the most hearty manner.

LIST OF PROFESSIONAL EXPERTS.

JAS. HAMILL, D. V. S., 416 E. 14th St. New York City, formerly Lecturer on Shoeing and diseases of the Foot in Col. Vet. Col., Pres't Nat'l Vet'y Med. Ass'n, now Prof. of Oper. Surg'y and Horse Shoeing, N. Y. Col. of Vet. Sur. and Sch. of Com. Med.

CHAS. A. MEYER,[*] D. V. S., Editor Veterinary Gazette, New York.

JOHN A. McLAUGHLIN, D. V. S., Providence, R. I., ex-Veterinary Inspector N. J. State Board of Health.

D. G. SUTHERLAND, V. S., East Saginaw, Mich., ex-Pres't Mich. State Vet'y Ass'n.

PAUL PAQUIN, M. D., V. S., Columbia, Mo., Prof. Compar. Med., Direct. Exper. Labratory, State Vet'y Inspector, and Pres't Mo. Ass'n of Vet'y Science and Compar. Medicine.

T. BENT COTTON, M. D., V. S., Mt. Vernon, O., Pres't Ohio State Vet'y Ass'n, Vice-Pres't Nat'l Vet'y Med. Ass'n.

DR. B. C. McBETH, Battle Creek, Mich., Sec'y Mich. State Vet'y Ass'n, Hon. Mem. N. Y. St. Acad. of Science and Com. Path.

J. A. DELL, V. S., Ann Arbor, Mich., Pres't Mich. State Vet'y Ass'n.

A. J. CHANDLER, V. S., Detroit, Mich., Vice-Pres't Mich. State Vet'y Ass'n.

S. BRENTON, V. S., Jackson, Mich., Ex-Pres't Mich. State Vet'y Ass'n.

WM. JOPLING, V. S., Owosso, Mich., Treasurer Mich. State Vet'y Ass'n.

A. I. ROOT, Medina, O., author of "A B C of Bee Culture."

JOHN A. ADAMS, Horticulturist, Battle Creek, Mich.

---

[*] Deceased while this was being put in type.

INTRODUCTION.

The following explanations I deem also necessary in connection with the reference to these gentlemen :—

Dr. Cotton was highly recommended to me as a man of much ability in the profession, by a prominent Eastern practitioner, and reference was made to his position among his *confrères* in the State, as assurance of his fitness for the work desired.

Dr. Paquin was known to me personally as a man of much more than ordinary attainments, and I made a special request that he would take charge of one or two of the more important departments. I am especially indebted to him also for translations from the French of analytical descriptions of the structure of the foot, he being known to me as an exceptionally fine French scholar.

I am also specially indebted to Dr. Meyer, not only for special papers, but for translations from the German on the structure of the foot, in which language he was a proficient scholar. In this respect, also, Dr. Hamill rendered me an exceptionally important service. Dr. Paquin, my best French scientific translator, was absent in Paris, engaged in special microscopic studies, and being unable to find a man competent to do the work, I explained the difficulty to Dr. Hamill, who stated that he would himself try to do it for me, and, to my surprise, I found him remarkably proficient, he being able to trace out readily every minute definition from the original, and adapt the explanations to the English, showing himself to be one of the most thorough scientific students of the structure of the foot in the veterinary profession.

Having personal acquaintance with Dr. Sutherland, who was at the time President of the Michigan State Veterinary Association, it occurred to me to send him sample chapters of the matter prepared, for his examination at the annual meeting of the Association at Jackson, and request him to refer me to those among the members of the Association competent and willing to take part in the work ; and through his aid, as well as that of the Secretary of the Association, Dr. Mc Beth, who also co-operated with me most cordially, I was able to secure the assistance of Drs. Dell, Chandler, Brenton, and Jopling, and Prof. Grange, of the Agricultural College.

The matter was now divided into sections and distributed to each of these experts, with freedom to make any changes or additions to the text they might deem necessary to make it most reliable and practical for reference. It was specially requested that the matter should be free from needless technicalities, and embody the most useful facts for the benefit of the class of readers for whom the work was intended. With the view of making this work as reliable as possible, special parts on the more malignant diseases were submitted to two or three in succession.

After the copy thus distributed had been all returned and put in type, it occurred to me that it would be a feature of special interest to my readers, to have the portraits of these professional friends engraved and placed in the work; and I was so fortunate (in some instances only after considerable persuasion) as to obtain permission to do so from those whose portraits are given; and I take great pleasure in presenting them as a good representation of the class of men engaged at present in the veterinary profession.

It is proper in this connection to state that should there appear any minor errors in the text, the responsibility for them must be entirely assumed by the author, as it was not possible, except at great inconvenience, after the matter had been put in type, to submit proofs to the gentlemen who had aided me in this work.

I may mention also that I made it a special object to have every detail of the work as fully and thoroughly illustrated as I could, as well as to include such features as would be most useful to the farmer. In carrying out this purpose I inserted in the stock department the large number of 800 figures, and in the horse department the still larger number of 950, among which are eighteen elegant plates. It is only necessary to state that there is no work heretofore published of this description that has more than a fourth of this number, and these usually of a very indifferent character, while this comprises the enormous aggregate, as will be seen, of 1,700, all having special reference to the text.

Particular attention is directed to the large number of illustrations of parasites common to the domestic animals; the great variety of figures illustrating the different diseases; the diversity of breeds of stock, particularly dairy cattle, sheep, hogs, and poultry. Certainly no work yet published can show any approach to the large number and varied character of the illustrations in these respects.

Interesting features will also be found in chapters on the Dog, on Bee-culture, the Growth of Fruit, including Insects Injurious to Fruit, and a Plea for the Birds, showing their value to the farmer.

The chapter on Bees, and that on the Protection of Fruit and Fruit Trees, will be found particularly interesting and valuable. That on Bee-culture was prepared with special care, under the supervision of A. I. ROOT, Esq., author of "The A B C of Bee Culture," and the highest authority on the subject, and includes the largest number of illustrations for the space occupied, that has yet been given on bees.

INTRODUCTION.

The chapter on Fruit was prepared by a leading horticulturist of large experience, MR. JOHN A. ADAMS, and will be found of great value and importance. The large number of fine and varied illustrations in this chapter, showing the insects that injure and destroy fruit, cannot but be of great interest, and with the text comprises knowledge of the greatest value to fruit-growers. I would call especial attention to this chapter, not only as a new feature, but for the practical character of its instructions and suggestions.

The Plea for the Birds should be read by every person of humane instincts. This paper is embodied mainly from an address by the famous and lamented REV. HENRY WARD BEECHER. This address was listened to by the author years before his death, and long before this work was prepared; but it struck him as so beautiful and valuable in every part, that he went at once to the stenographer and engaged him to furnish a copy for his special use. The addition of this chapter was in a good degree owing to suggestions of leading officers of the American Humane Society. This will be found one of the most interesting features of this work, because most useful and elevating in its influence, and being one of the finest pleas for the birds ever written, showing their value to the farmer, and the duty of protecting them. THE AUTHOR.

THE STANDARD
Horse and Stock Book.

Chapter I.

PRELIMINARY REMARKS.

Fig. 1.— Ideal Head of an Intelligent, Docile Character.

ONCE, while stopping with a farmer, as a matter of amusement I took a colt that had become unmanageable to him, and made him perfectly gentle. Upon learning what I had done, the farmer was so surprised at the result as to offer me fifty dollars for the secret. Without thinking, I proposed teaching him and ten of his neighbors how I did it, in addition to other points that might be of interest to them. In this I was entirely successful, and thus I was unintentionally drifted into the most trying and exacting field of effort that ever man engaged in, which continued nearly nineteen years. I was necessarily forced into contact with all sorts of people, who were continually trying to break me down, and in addition I had the most vicious and difficult horses forced upon me to experiment upon; and that I succeeded at all seems to me even now so remarkable as to be beyond belief. But without realizing it, or knowing it at the time, the people who forced

26 PRELIMINARY REMARKS.

me to these trials were in reality my best friends, because proving the best instructors to me in the world ; and the experiments upon vicious horses were just what was necessary to give me the best opportuni-

FIGS. 2–4.—Extremes of Vicious Character.

ties of observation and practice needed to master the subject. Now, in teaching classes I soon found it necessary to make such explanations of points and conditions as I could before making experiments ; and in like manner, before taking up the details of instruction, I think it necessary to refer to such points as will be most suggestive in the study of the subject. I may state that this is somewhat difficult here, because compelled to limit my explanations to less than one half of what I have been able to devote to it in my regular work on the horse, and also to omit many chapters of much interest to the general reader.

Many of the lower animals possess some qualities by nature that make them, in some respects, really superior to man. The dog, for example, can follow the track of his master through a crowd of strangers, though hours behind, and find him ; and he will also find his way home, though distant hundreds of miles—a fact that has been repeatedly proved. The ordinary sheep-dog will at command find and bring home stray sheep of the flock ; and the blood-hound can perform the still more remarkable feat of taking up the track of a criminal hours afterward, by the scent of a bit of his clothing, and pick him out from hundreds of others who had been his companions—a power that entitles even the commonest cur to our kindest consideration. The eagle and vulture, though miles in the

FIG. 5.—A Portrait of a Docile Family Horse.

PRELIMINARY REMARKS.

Fig. 6.—A very Intelligent, Docile Character.

air, can see the smallest objects of prey on the ground—a power far beyond that of man. Thus these superior qualities, exhibited so largely by the lower animals, seem to be a special provision of nature to guard them from danger and aggression, or to aid them in providing sustenance.

Now, this singular power of instinct appears to be a very strongly marked feature of the horse's nature. The wild horse of the prairie cannot be approached near enough on the windward side to imperil his safety; and even when cornered and unable to get away, his acts of biting, striking, or kicking are but his natural promptings to defend himself. It is also seen that no matter how wild a colt, when treated with such kindness as to win his confidence, he not only will not show fear of man, but become a pet. A good demonstration of this is shown in the remarkable docility of the Arab horses, which are always treated with the utmost kindness; and ladies who are specially kind to horses, it is known, can approach them anywhere, and make them such pets that they will follow, even into the house. Perhaps in no way is this peculiar instinct more strikingly shown than in the repugnance of exceptionally sensitive, intelligent horses to men who may be ignorantly or thoughtlessly cruel to them.

Fig. 7.—Intelligent, Courageous, but very Sensitive Nature.

Hence it is evident that the true ground of success in the subjection and education of the horse, or in breaking up and overcoming bad habits when formed, must be in proportion to the degree to which the efforts can be intelligently addressed to the line of these instincts, holding passive, combating, or overcoming them while addressing the understanding, without exciting his fears or resistance; and it is absolutely imperative that in his education these conditions should not be disregarded.

Another point: a horse may be moved to intense excitement and extreme resistance by even a momentary impression of fear, without any contact with or cause for feeling direct physical pain; and again, in like manner, when properly treated, such fear may be overcome without resorting to treatment that would cause the least physical pain or injury.

FIG. 8.—One of the most Vicious Horses ever Subdued by the Author.

Another important feature for consideration is the wonderful adaptation in the various domestic animals, not only to the several wants and requirements of man, but to the sections of the world in which we find them. Thus, for example, the Esquimau has not only a dog, but one peculiarly fitted by nature to his especial wants, acting not only as a fisherman and a hunter, but as a beast of burden, being in fact the only animal that could live and be of any use to him so far north. A little farther south, the Laplander has the reindeer, that lives on the moss peculiar to those regions, providing both sustenance and clothing for him, as well as being the very best means of traveling over those dreary, frozen plains. The Peruvians have the llama for carrying burdens over the Andes. The Arabs have the camel for their peculiar want, that of traveling over the arid, sandy

FIG. 9.—Nervous, Excitable Horse.

desert, and so constituted as to carry within himself a supply of water sufficient to last for many days.

Not only do we see here special families, demonstrating this principle most strikingly, but such subdivisions of each as adapt them more perfectly for special uses. Now the horse, which is by far the most noble, valuable, and useful of all the domestic animals, in the management of which we are specially interested, shows this to a wonderful degree in size, disposition, and intelligence. For slow, drudging work, we have the coarse-grained, patient, heavy cart or plow horse, while for quick, long-continued exertion, we have the lithe thoroughbred, with the conformation of the greyhound, capable, if necessary, of running with the fleetness of the wind. From these extremes we have illimitable modifications, adapting them the more perfectly to the various requirements of man. Now, it is clear that the nervous, energetic racer or thoroughbred would be entirely out of place for the cart or plow, and the coarse-grained cart or plow horse for the quick, active exertion of speedy travel; and that to make each most useful he must be employed for such work only as nature best fits him for.

FIG. 10.—A Vicious, Treacherous Nature.

FIG. 11.—Portrait of a Noted Vicious Horse.

Dependent upon these physical conditions are others that have a still more important bearing upon the success of our efforts, because they are necessarily more obscure, and we are compelled to study them more carefully to win success, namely, the intelligence and disposition of horses.

To illustrate my meaning in part: It is clear that some horses

FIG. 12.—Sullen Treachery.

are very much more intelligent and quick to comprehend than others; that some are by nature of the most perfect docility, while others have a large element of the naturally vicious, dangerous character. Here, then, we are compelled to study and learn, if possible, two things,—the conditions requisite for the best management of the sensitive, intelligent nature, as well as those that are dull, strong, and naturally vicious.

In the first, we must study how to address and win the understanding directly, if possible, without a ruffle of excitement; and in the management of the second, we must impress the intelligence in such a way as to win obedience most safely and easily.

This necessarily requires the careful study of the vital powers, dependent upon the following conditions: First, the intelligence, as dependent upon the volume of brain; second, the physical strength, as dependent upon size and quality of bodily structure; third, the peculiar phase and degree of the viciousness.

It is evident that when we have large brain, dense texture of body, good digestion, and large, deep chest, we have indicated, first, great natural strength; second, great endurance, in consequence of ability to assimilate food; third, capacity to oxygenate the blood rapidly, thus giving great endurance for long-sustained effort. Lacking these conditions to any extent, even though there

FIG. 13.—Sketch from Life of the most Vicious Mustang Pony the Writer ever Saw.

may be great energy and pluck, there will be less ability to resist well-sustained coercive measures.

Now, dependent upon the order of intelligence and bodily structure are certain peculiarities. For example, a full forehead, large, clear eyes, tending to brown in color, set well out on the head, eyelids thin, medium length from eyes to ears, ears pointed and of medium length, placed not very wide apart and high between them, and large nostrils,

FIG. 14.—Sketch of a Vicious Stallion.

will most always indicate the intelligent, steady, reliable, family horse; while a forehead rather narrow, small, round eyes, set well back in the side of the head, eyelids heavy, long from eyes to ears, ears long and flabby, with a tendency to throw them back a little, nose rounding, and nostrils small, show the opposite, or a dull, sullen, treacherous nature. If the forehead be of a medium or good breadth, the eyes good size, clear, and setting well out, the lids thin, short from eyes to ears, ears a little longer than common, and nostrils large, there will be indicated intelligence, activity, but great sensibility; usually termed the nervous, sensitive horse, that will not bear excitement.

FIG. 15.—Portrait of a Noted Vicious Horse in a Rage.

From these extremes, again, we have illimitable modifications, dependent upon conditions referred to.

Figs. 1, 5, 6, and 7 give the best expressions of a naturally docile, intelligent character. Figs. 1, 5, and 6 are fine illustrations of the best types of the gentle family horse. Fig. 7 is the best type of a sensitive, but very intelligent horse, being a portrait of a noted Arabian horse. Fig. 9 is a good type of a very nervous, sensitive character. Figs. 8, 10, and 11

FIG. 16.—Naturally Docile and Intelligent.

are modifications of the dull, sullen, treacherous type. Fig. 10 is a portrait of a very marked case. Fig. 11 is also a portrait of a very noted vicious horse. Fig. 13 is that of a mustang pony, the most desperate, reckless creature the writer ever subjected to treatment. Fig. 17 is a portrait of a case that up to nine years old had proved utterly unmanageable, but whose character was made so gentle, after an hour's treatment, that it was afterward used as a family horse. Fig. 21 is a good illustration of the barnyard lunkhead. In addition there is seen to be a large number of illustrations showing combinations and contrasts of character which are deserving of careful study.

The size of bone, the texture of bodily structure, the length and color of hair, amount of hair in mane or tail, the action in moving, the size and expression of eye, the peculiarity of head, its length, breadth, etc., are subjects requiring the most constant and careful consideration in directing intelligent treatment.

Principles of Treatment.

In the subjection and education of horses, we have several natural difficulties to contend with. First: The horse is much stronger than man, and just so far as he in any way learns that he can resist man's control, to that degree will he be encouraged and inclined to resist or combat him; hence, an in-

FIG. 17.—"Wild Pete." A Very Peculiar and Interesting Case.

dispensable condition of his successful education is that he must be given no opportunity to learn that he is not in every respect subordinate to man in physical power, until his character becomes fixed.

Fig. 18.—Docile, Intelligent.

Second: His methods of reasoning being dependent upon and limited to the observation and experience of his senses of seeing, hearing, smelling, and feeling, to prevent his becoming excited or frightened at objects and sounds with which he is necessarily brought in contact, he must be convinced in his own way, through these faculties, of their harmless and innocent character. Consequently, if he be treated according to these laws of his nature, he can be made to do willingly, without fear or resistance, anything for which he is by nature adapted.

Third: The horse, being unable to understand the meaning of articulated language, excepting so far as words are associated with actions, we must address his intelligence on this plane of his reasoning, because it is only by doing so that he can be expected to comprehend our wishes clearly.

Fourth: To the degree that the horse becomes excited, frightened, or confused, he must necessarily be both unable to understand what is required to be done, and correspondingly less inclined to submit to restraint in his management. Hence, whatever the treatment, it must be of a character not to confuse or excite him, nor to expose him to such excessive fear as would shock and derange his nervous system.

Taking these conditions in order, we see, for example, that if a horse learns to pull

Fig. 19.—A Noted Vicious Horse.

away, break his halter, resist the blacksmith in shoeing, or run away, etc., he will be encouraged to and try to do so afterward until the habit becomes fixed. On the contrary, when a colt is first haltered, no matter how hard he may resist, if once taught to submit, he will not only readily follow without restraint, but will do so ever afterward; or when the feet are taken up and handled until the operation is fully submitted to, or such restraint brought upon him as to compel submission, there will not only be obedience for the time, but all inclination to resist will be radically overcome.

FIG. 20.—**Strong-Willed, Intelligent Character.**

Now, the principle is the same in relation to other habits, or in overcoming viciousness. No matter how wild or unmanageable the horse may be, if he can be so treated that successful resistance becomes impossible, and he is shown that he will not be injured, there will not only be entire submission without the use of force, but if not excited or abused, he will remain permanently docile.

But it is imperative that there be at no point such an exposure of weakness as would encourage resistance; for, though the method of treatment may be in itself right, if not carried to the point desired, the difficulties of the treatment will necessarily be increased to a degree liable to precipitate failure. For example, there may be strength to take up a colt's foot; but if at any point of holding it it is pulled away, and control resisted, he will be inclined to resist afterward with as much energy as if there had not been sufficient power to take it up at all. Or, in teaching a horse to lead by the halter, if he resists successfully it will teach him to resist the efforts by pulling away. Now,

FIG. 21.—**Barnyard Lunkhead.**

the method of pulling on the halter may be all right, but the point of difficulty would be in not having power to carry it far enough. Not only this, but it is vital to success to do it properly, or in such

PRINCIPLES OF TREATMENT. 35

a way that there would be the least inclination to resistance. If, for example, in taking up the horse's foot, by standing forward of the hip, well up near the body, facing backward, one hand is rested against the hip, while at

Fig. 22.—Docile Expression.   Fig. 23.—Docile Expression.

the moment of taking up the foot with the other, there is firm pressure exerted against the hip, to throw the weight upon the opposite leg, the foot can be brought up easily, and then, when submitted to, the simple movement forward will bring it against the knees to be handled with safety as desired. In leading by the halter, if, instead of pulling straight ahead, which gives the horse great advantage to resist, the operator stands opposite the shoulder and pulls sufficiently hard to bring the horse off his feet a few times, he will soon follow unconditionally without the least restraint.

In a hundred different ways this principle is seen to be illustrated in consequence of the horse's not being sufficiently disciplined to make him entirely manageable in harness and fearless when under the tests of severe excitement. It is for this reason that horses that may have been driven for months, or even years, when managed with care, or not subjected to unusual causes of accident or excitement, are liable at some unguarded moment, when

Fig. 24.—Coarse, Low-bred Horse.

exposed to some exceptional strain, up to which they have not been tested, to become frightened and resist control, thereby resulting in constantly recurring cases of accident, as well as endangering the spoiling of the horse; which would all have been prevented by the application and proper carrying out of necessary treatment in the first place.

Second: We see that when an object of fear or unusual sound is brought suddenly or unexpectedly to the horse's notice, or in contact with any part of his body, it is liable to excite the most intense fear and resistance; whereas, if brought slowly and gently to his notice, letting him smell or feel of it until convinced of its harmlessness, it can be brought over and around him without causing the least fear or attracting his attention. It makes no difference whether

Fig. 25.—Vicious.

Fig. 26.—Treacherous.

it is in driving to a carriage, letting the cross-piece come against the quarters, raising an umbrella behind him, the noise of a steam-engine, or anything else, the principle is the same.

Third: In relation to making him understand the meaning of special sounds or words of command. If a man were simply to repeat the word "Whoa" to a horse, he might do it indefinitely without his being able to understand its meaning and object. But if the horse were moved moderately, and immediately after the command he were pulled upon hard enough to make him stop, he would in a short time, when the word is repeated, learn to stop to avoid being hurt. Or, in teaching him to back, if after the word is spoken the reins be pulled upon sufficiently to force him back, he will, after a few repetitions, learn, when the command is given, to go back freely, to evade the restraint and pain.

The better to illustrate this I will include here the details of teaching a few tricks.

PRINCIPLES OF TREATMENT.

To teach a horse to make a bow, first prick him lightly on the back with a pin, and repeat this until, in his efforts to avoid the annoyance, he drops his head, after which caress him, repeating the pricking until the head is again dropped, when again repeat the caress and give him something of which he is fond, and continue to alternate in this way with the pricking, caressing, and rewarding, until at the least motion of the hand toward the back he will drop his head.

To teach him to kick, simply prick him on the rump until there is an inclination to kick up, when, as before, caress him, and so repeat until the least motion of the hand toward the rump will induce him to kick up.

In teaching any kind or number of tricks, the principle is the same, the only difference being that instead of a pin, other means adapted to the requirements of the case must be used.

But one thing should be taught at a time, and that slowly and carefully repeated until thoroughly understood. The duller the horse, and the more complicated or difficult to the understanding the point to be taught, the less can be safely attempted, and the more time must necessarily be taken ; while the more intelligent the horse, and the simpler the thing required to be done, the more can be accomplished. And each point thus made should be made the foundation for the next, until the education is complete.

Again, to have prompt obedience, the same signal and word given in teaching the trick, or whatever is required to be done, must be repeated exactly, *even to the tone and pitch of the voice;* otherwise a horse is liable

FIGS. 27-30.—Modifications of Good Character.

FIGS. 31-36.—Extremes of Low-bred, Vicious Character.

to become more or less confused and unable to understand or obey. The principle is the same in teaching a horse to do anything in or out of harness; the point being that such means or methods of treatment are to be used as will give the necessary control, and at the same time convey to the understanding in the most direct manner the idea of what is desired to be done.

Now, the principle is exactly the same in both preventing and overcoming viciousness or bad habits, no matter what their character or degree; the only difference being that instead of teaching a trick, or obedience in any respect, we must aim now to combat the habit already formed, simply repeating until there is entire docility and submission.

Again, in resorting to physical power, the nearer we are able to use it so as not to cause pain nor excite the belligerent nature of the horse, the better. If a man were strong enough to take a fighting bully by the shoulders and shake him so thoroughly as to show him that he had power to control the fellow as he pleased, and then treat him kindly and convince him that his intentions were good, it would have a better effect in impressing him with a sense of the man's mastery, and make him less inclined to resist, than if he had obtained control of him after a desperate struggle that would heat his blood and arouse his passions to the point of recklessness.

In like manner, if we could use power directly upon a horse, so as to restrain and control him as we wished, it would be far more effective than if the effort were of a character to cause him to become maddened and heated; or, if this be impossible, then the resorting to such indirect measures of coercion as will enable us to accomplish this most safely and easily.

Now, the treatment herein given does this

PRINCIPLES OF TREATMENT. 39

with far more ease, directness, and success than has ever yet been accomplished. It not only enables us to control with the greatest facility, frequently in a few minutes, not exceeding twenty or thirty, horses that had resisted all previous efforts to subdue or control them, and become practically worthless, but it gives the proper foundation for making the character safe and reliable afterward, its most remarkable feature being the startling results accomplished in so short a time, apparently changing the entire nature of the horse as if by magic.

This treatment is the outgrowth of the practice of over eighteen years of the most constant and exacting experimenting, and has been proved, by the results exhibited, to bring the control and education of horses as nearly as possible to the line of an exact science, conclusively showing that when horses become vicious or unmanageable, it is the result of ignorance or bad management, which the treatment herein given, if properly applied, would have entirely prevented.

I could include a great deal of other treatment, and much of it very good, but wishing only to give what is practical, I confine myself to such treatment only as I have found in my experience to be best.

Before taking up details, I would state that there is no difficulty in making a horse, even when of a very vicious character, gentle for a short time; but the difficulty is to be able to hold and fix the character in such a way that he will remain gentle. This may be done in quite a variety of ways. Any method of lowering the vitality, such as bleeding, physicking, preventing sleep, depriving of food or water, subjecting to intense pain, or, in fact, any means whereby we can successfully lower the strength, will make a horse gentle. But the difficulty is that, however gentle he may be at the time, when the

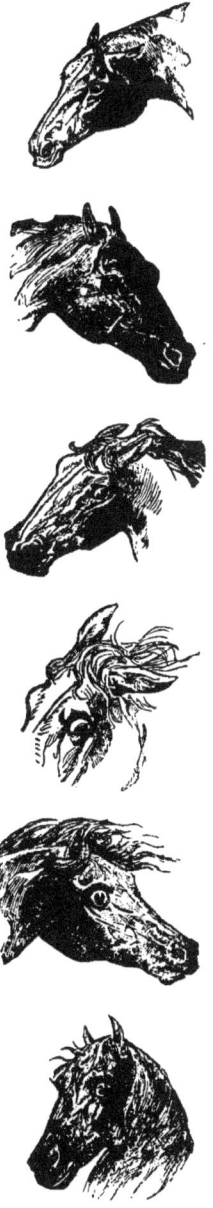

FIGS. 37-42. — Modifications of Well-bred Character.

Figs. 43–48. — Modifications of Vicious Character.

effect passes off, or the horse regains his strength, there will be so great a tendency to gravitate back to the former condition that the treatment will nearly always result in disappointment.

While it is known that many persons have the power of controlling the will of others, or what is termed psychologizing them, and that some of the lower animals secure their prey in this manner, as exhibited by the snake in charming birds and small animals, various cases of which I refer to (particularly in discussing this subject) in my special work on the horse, the principle does not seem to work in the control of horses; certainly it has not in my experience, and I have hundreds of times produced results before classes which seemed so remarkable to them that they would insist upon searching my gloves and clothes for some scent or odor which might account to them for the effect produced; and even after this they could scarcely realize that it could be accomplished by the treatment illustrated before them. I have had members of classes repeatedly tell me in private that they knew I must have acquired my power by some secret not revealed to them, and be so confident of this that they would offer me large sums for it.

I necessarily acquired a certain expertness, the result of practice and accuracy of judgment in applying treatment, that often enabled results, in the control of certain types of resistance and character, that seemed very remarkable. This was frequently shown in the cases of horses afraid of a blanket, a buffalo-robe, or something of the kind; in the control of a stallion so as to be led up to a mare and then called away; the control of a wild and seemingly very dangerous colt that had been proved very unmanageable, so as to drive entirely gentle without breeching; the making of a colt follow, or the making of a halter-puller when hitched stand quietly without attempting to pull. It was no unusual thing for me to do, when the case happened to be good, within two or three minutes to be able to

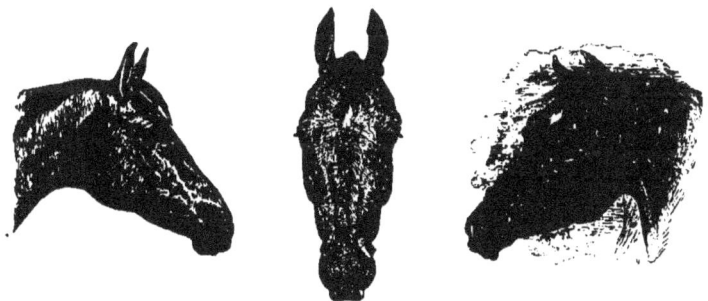

FIGS. 49-51 —Three Types of Good Character.

throw a buffalo-robe as I pleased over the head or around the body of a horse that had previously been quite seriously afraid of it, without the horse caring much about it. In the control of a head-strong stallion, if a good subject, it rarely required more than four or five minutes ; the hitching up and driving gentle of such a colt as described, in six to eight or ten minutes ; the making of a halter-puller stand submissive under the most severe excitement of being

FIGS. 52-54.—Coarse, Low Character.

whipped over the head, or the cause of the pulling thrown in his face, without his pulling, in a couple of minutes.

Now, it is needless to add that if this treatment had been applied roughly or improperly, this control could only be obtained after considerable severe treatment that would excite the horse greatly, thus acquiring control only at the expense of considerable time

Fig. 55.—Vicious Horse in a Rage.

and trouble. This rule, in fact, runs through every phase of the treatment, in illustrating its success and applying it properly.

SUGGESTIONS IN RELATION TO PRINCIPLES OF MANAGEMENT.

If we tie down a horse's ear, or grasp it with the hand and twist it a little, it will be found that a horse that had been very nervous to shoe will often stand quite gentle to be shod. The jockey has learned that he can frequently make a bad kicking mare drive without kicking by tying the tail down to the crosspiece of the shafts or forward to the belly-band of the harness, so that it cannot be raised; because disabling the tail creates such a sense of helplessness as to counteract the inclination to kick.

Sometimes checking the head high will accomplish the same result. Putting cobbles or shot in the ears will, on the same principle, sufficiently disconcert a balky horse to make him go right along. Blindfolding by covering the eyes only carries this to a greater extent, and will be found in most cases to make quite a stubborn horse work with excellent success.

Fig. 56.—A Noted Vicious Horse.

PRINCIPLES OF TREATMENT.

The secret of the first horse-tamer of whom I have any account —Dick Christian of England—consisted simply in tying up the fore leg, and then mounting and riding the horse until submissive. The next step in this direction was disabling both fore legs, and thus forcing the horse to lie down, which carried this principle to a greater degree of perfection. This was regarded a very rare secret, and was the basis of the methods practiced by Bull in England, Sullivan in Mallow, Ireland, Denton Offutt in Kentucky, and O. H. P. Fancher in Ohio, who were the first, most pretentious, and noted, before the advent of Rarey, who learned the secret of Denton Offutt,

FIG. 57.—An Incident in the Driving of a Noted Runaway Horse.

at the time a resident of Georgetown, Ky. This was the sole and only secret upon which were based Rarey's most extraordinary pretensions, and for teaching which he made $100,000 in England; and probably much more than that was paid in this country for the same knowledge.

I may add, by way of explanation, that the control of Cruiser and other noted cases in England and France, upon which his reputation was based, although it was assumed to be, was not and could not have been accomplished by this treatment. Those interested in a full explanation of all the facts in regard to it, will find the details in the chapter on "Subjection" in my work, " Facts for Horse-Owners."

44 PRINCIPLES OF TREATMENT.

Various remedies have also been assumed to be used for taming horses under the pretense of a great secret, or the guise of fascination, on the principle of using certain scents for attracting and controlling certain wild animals or fishes. These means have about the same effect upon a horse as good apples, or anything else of which the horse is naturally fond. While it is true that horses may sometimes, for example, be strongly repelled by blood or the odor of poisonous snakes, and other dangerous animals, and that they are attracted and quieted by other scents, I have found nothing of the

FIG. 58.—The Famous Horse Jet, of Portland, Me., Subdued by the Author in Thirty Minutes.

kind that would accomplish satisfactory results to me in their control, but little more than would be done by good apples, or the giving of anything else of which the horse is fond. Offutt and Fancher, before referred to, were the most pretentious in their use of such scents, the details of which I include in my other work.

Various alterations or modifications of this method of subduing horses were made at different times by different parties; but it was not until I was able to bring into use that here described as the First Method of Subjection, that the real power and effect of this principle of treatment was practically brought out; which has been the outgrowth of a great deal of practical experimenting requiring over fifteen years' time.

If in wrestling a man could be thrown directly upon his back as fast as he could get up, it is evident a much more effectual impression of his antagonist's mastery could be made than if he were permitted to carry on a doubtful struggle for half an hour, that would only occasionally bring him to his knees. The very doubtfulness of the contest would stimulate him to the utmost resistance until exhausted. But if he could be thrown at once, and as often as he could get up, his courage and confidence would be soon broken up, convincing him of the uselessness of continuing the struggle, and making the impression of mastery all that could be desired.

FIG. 59.—An Act of a Noted Vicious Stallion Subdued by the Author in Less than an Hour.

Now, the effect upon a horse will be the same. If the control can be made direct and positive, throwing him on his side as often as he can get up, the confidence which stimulates the resistance is quickly broken up.

The method here given as the First Method of Subjection, bears exactly this relation to that formerly used. It gives just the advantage and power that will enable any ordinary man to throw the strongest horse as quickly and as often as he can get up; in addition, he can hold him down or roll him back, as he pleases, thereby making it not only far more effective, but entirely obviating the objections to the old method.

I have called attention to these interesting facts: first, that the horse is governed in his actions by certain instincts or inherent powers, and that these must be studied closely as the foundation of his successful management; next, tha, these constitutional differences are only provisions adapting him for special uses; and that his character is clearly shown by the peculiarities of his bodily structure, actions, and more especially by the features of the head. This will show, when looked at carefully, that resistance is only the expression of natural instinct, and that fear or vicious actions are not to be taken as indicating a degree of bad character or viciousness that should

FIG. 60.—**The Thorough-bred.**

be considered an obstacle in making the character good, simply requiring greater care and thought in meeting and combating the resistance, whatever it is, in the most simple, direct, and humane manner. Though referred to before, it is so important that I call attention to it again here, that though the treatment may be applied just right, if not carried far enough, the failure may be as great as if improper treatment had been used; and above all, that the better nature is to be won by patient, persistent kindness. I have called attention, next, to the various methods of treatment taught me by the experience of many long years of observation, experiment, and study, and have tried faithfully to make the explanations as simple and plain as I could. .

PRINCIPLES OF TREATMENT.

Now, it is indispensable that this chapter, at least certain parts of it, which are the key and groundwork of the detailed

FIG. 61.—**A Good Model of Draught Horse.**

instructions in subsequent chapters, should be read very carefully. You cannot understand these principles too well.

FIG. 62.—**Shetland Pony.**

PRINCIPLES OF TREATMENT.

There are also many points having close relation to this subject, and of great interest to the horseman, which want of space in a general work of this character compels me to omit: First, the inside history of Rarey's career, as a means of correcting the false impressions created by his pretensions and assumed success, because without it there was necessarily a certain mystery about the performance of this duty that could not well be made plain; second, the details

FIG. 63.—Model of the French Norman Horse.

of the management and history of a large number of specially representative vicious horses, as suggestive aids to treatment in similar cases; third, the outlines of my experience with reference to many cases and circumstances named, the better to authenticate the facts stated. There are also special chapters on other points having close and important connection with the instruction given on this subject. All these points are very fully given in my regular work on the horse, which can be referred to by those interested.

I would now call attention to what I deem the most important condition of success, which should be considered, above all others, as deserving of the most serious consideration, namely, the judgment and skill with which the treatment is applied.

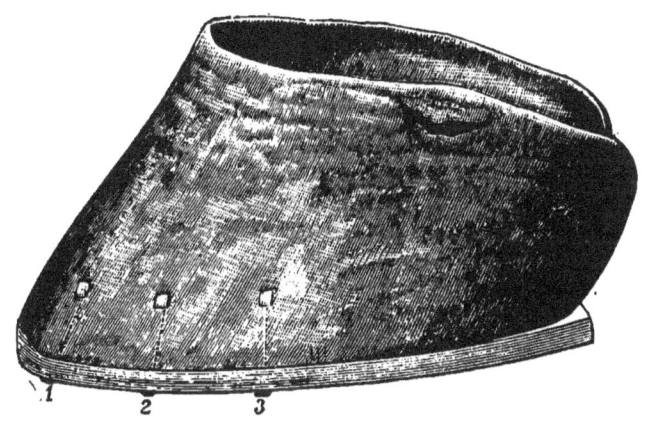

Fig. I.
The shoe properly formed, adjusted, and nailed on the hoof of a five-year-old horse that had never been shod but once.

Fig. II.
The foot as it is ruined by bad treatment. The shoe and nails are too large; the nails too many in number and driven too deep. The shoe is set back too far. The hoof is rasped away so much as to weaken it and destroy its symmetry.

PLATE I.

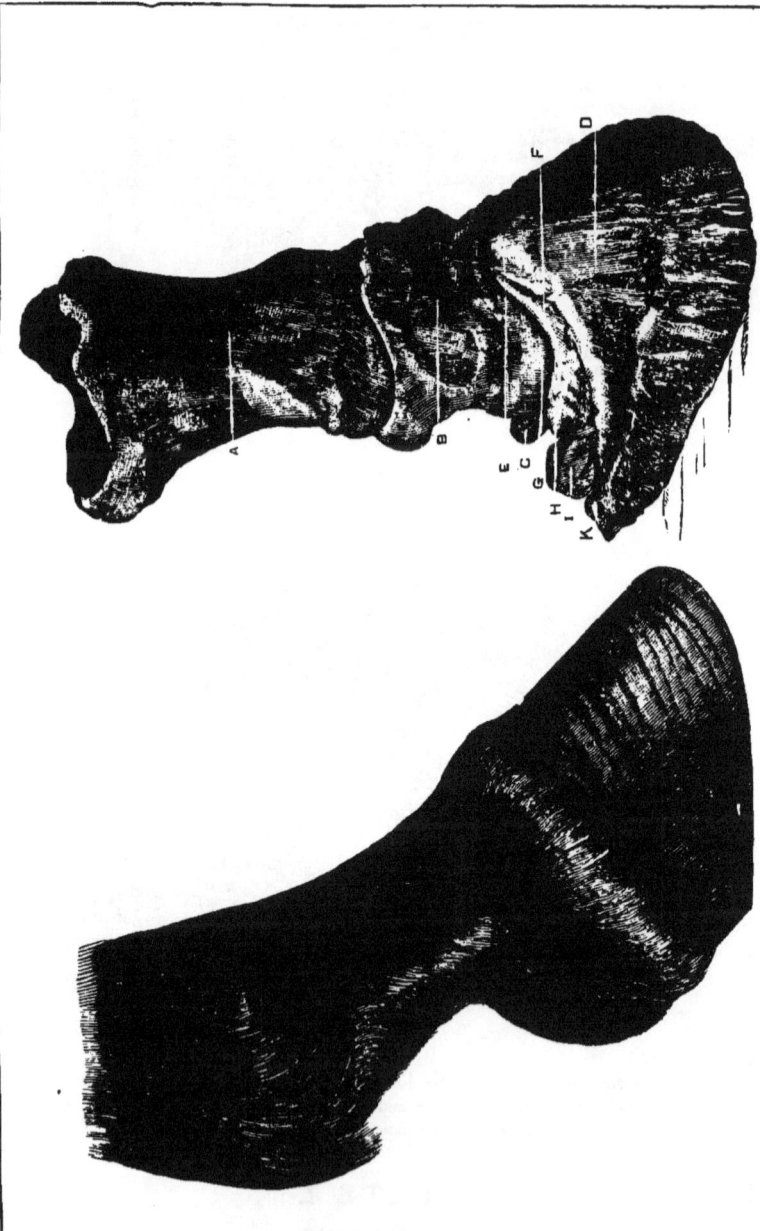

PLATE II.

PLATE II.*

A front view of the bones of the fore feet of a horse in their relative position.

- A. The pastern bone.
- B. The coronary bone.
- C. The navicular bone.
- D. The foot bone.
- E. The point of insertion of the tendon of the extensor muscle.
- F. A concavity to give attachment to the ligament which unites the foot bone to the coronary bone at G.
- G. Coronary bone. .
- H. A continuation of the same concavity, to which the cartilage of the foot bone is attached.
- I, I. The upper and lower processes of the foot bone.
- K, K. A groove in the foot bone, which receives a division of the main artery, coming round from behind.
- K, L. A groove receiving another division of that artery, which proceeds round the extreme edges of the foot bone.

---

*The plates here given are selected from the author's special book on the horse, "Facts for Horse Owners," in which are forty plates. In the extra edition these plates are printed in colors.

PLATE III.

PLATE III.

Fig. I.

A back view of the bones of the fore foot in their relative situation.

- A. Pastern bone.
- B. Coronary bone.
- C. Navicular bone.
- D. Foot bone.
- E. A cavity which in the natural state is filled with fat.
- F. The upper surface of the navicular bone, from which two ligaments arise, and pass round the lateral depression in the coronary bone, marked G.
- G. Points of attachment on each side of the ligament which unites the navicular bone to the foot bone.
- I. Two grooves in which two main trunks of the arteries are continued into the foot bone.
- K. The line of insertion of the tendon of the flexor muscle.

Fig. II.

A view of the anterior and inferior surfaces of the navicular bone detached from the other bones.

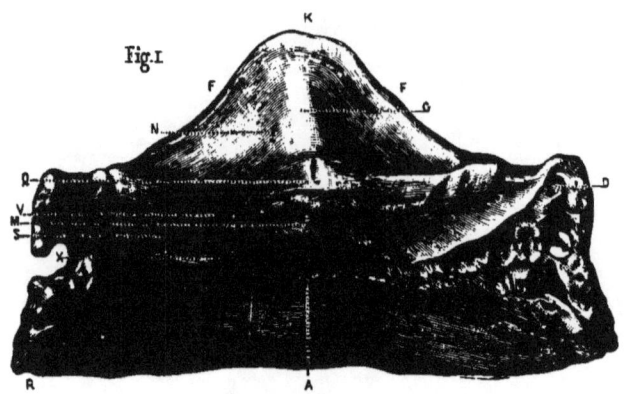

Fig. I.

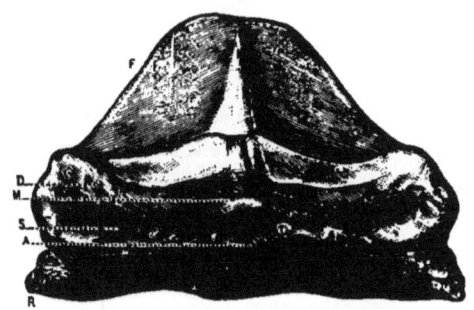

Fig. II.

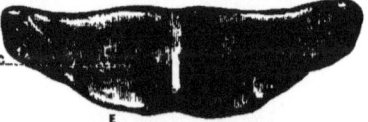

Fig. III.

Fig. IV.

Fig. V.

PLATE IV.

PLATE IV.

This cut represents the third phalanx seen from its posterior part; and the navicular bone,—inferior, superior, and anterior views.

Fig. I.
Posterior Part of the Third Phalanx (ADULT).

- A. Semi-lunar crest.
- D. Basilar process.
- F. Superior border.
- G. Spreading out of the articular face.
- K. Anterior view of the pyramidal eminence.
- M. Posterior view of the inferior face.
- N. Glenoid cavity of the superior face.
- Q. Portion of the articular surface corresponding to the anterior border of the navicular bone.
- R. Retrossal process.
- S. Edge of the plantar fissure.
- V. Posterior border of the third phalanx.
- X. Plantar orifice for passage of blood vessels.

Fig. II.
Posterior Part of the Third Phalanx (COLT).

- A. Semi-lunar crest.
- D. Basilar process.
- F. Superior border.
- M. Posterior view of the bone.
- R. Retrossal process.
- S. Plantar fissure.

Fig. III.
Inferior Face of Navicular.

- C. Transverse ridge.
- E. Anterior border.
- H. Extremity of the bone.

Fig. IV.
- A. Median ridge or bulge of the superior face.
- D. Anterior superior border.
- E. Anterior inferior border.
- G. Posterior border (is very thick, and cribbled or pierced with vascular orifices).

Fig. V.
Anterior Face of Navicular.

- E. Soft part hollowed under the anterior articular facet.
- H. Articular facet corresponding to the posterior facet of the third phalanx.

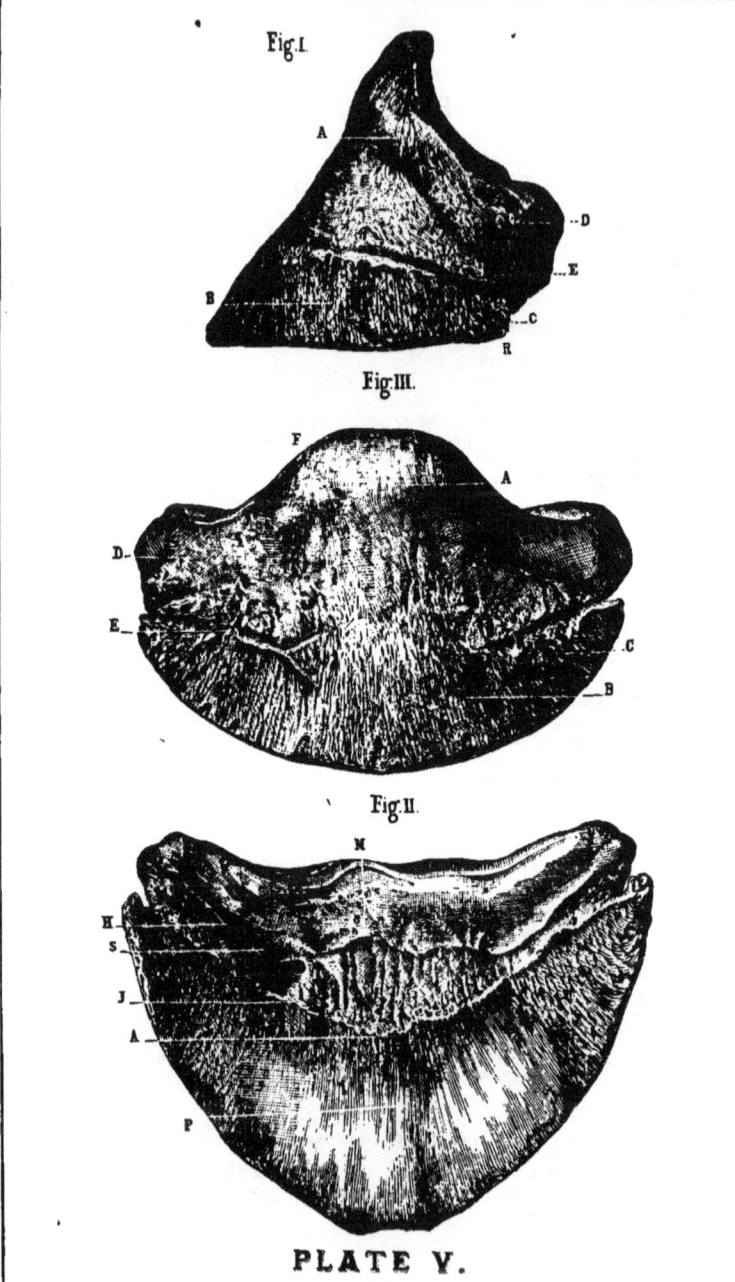

PLATE V.

PLATE V.

This plate represents the third phalanx of the colt, seen from its lateral, anterior, and inferior faces.

Fig. I.
Lateral Face.
- A. Base of the pyramidal eminence.
- B. Vascular porosities.
- C. Patilobe eminence.
- E. Pre-plantar fissure.
- D. Basilar process.
- K. Pyramidal eminence.
- R. Retrossal process.

Fig. II.
Anterior Face.
- A. Pyramidal eminence.
- B. Porosities and vascular imprints
- C. Patilobe eminence.
- D. Basilar process.
- E. Pre-plantar fissure.
- F. Superior border.

Fig. III.
Inferior Face.
- A. Semi-lunar crest.
- H. Plantar fissure.
- J. Imprint of the insertion of the perforaus.
- P. Inferior face.
- S. Edge of the plantar fissure.

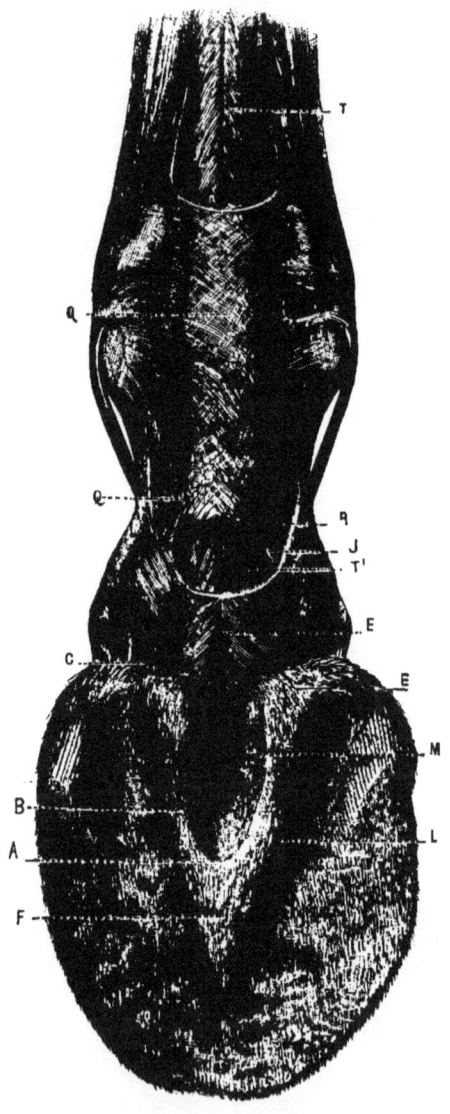

PLATE VI.

PLATE VI.

This figure represents the posterior face of the digital region, flexed backward in a manner to show in its full extent the inferior or plantar face of the foot.

The skin has been lifted from above the third phalanx, and the enveloping sheaths of the tendons are dissected. The velvety tissue is preserved.

- A. Median part of the pyramidal body (fleshy frog) of plantar cushion, or sensitive tissue of the sole.
- B. Branches of the pyramidal body.
- C. Cartilaginous bulb.
- E. Angle of inflection of the branches of the pyramidal body.
- F. Point or apex of the fleshy frog.
- J. Interval of separation of the two branches of the perforatus.
- L. Lateral lacunæ of the pyramidal body.
- M. Median lacunæ of the pyramidal body.
- Q, Q. Fibrous sheath of union of the two branches of the perforatus
- R. Branches of the perforatus directing th emselves towardtheir point of insertion at the second phalanx.
- T. Tendon of the perforatus.
- T'. Tendon of the perforans at its passage between the branches of the perforatus.
- V. Strengthening sheath of the plantar aponeurosis.
- X. Lateral bands of the strengthening sheath of the plantar aponeurosis, which cross the direction of the branches of the perforatus to go and attach themselves on the lateral parts of the first phalanx.

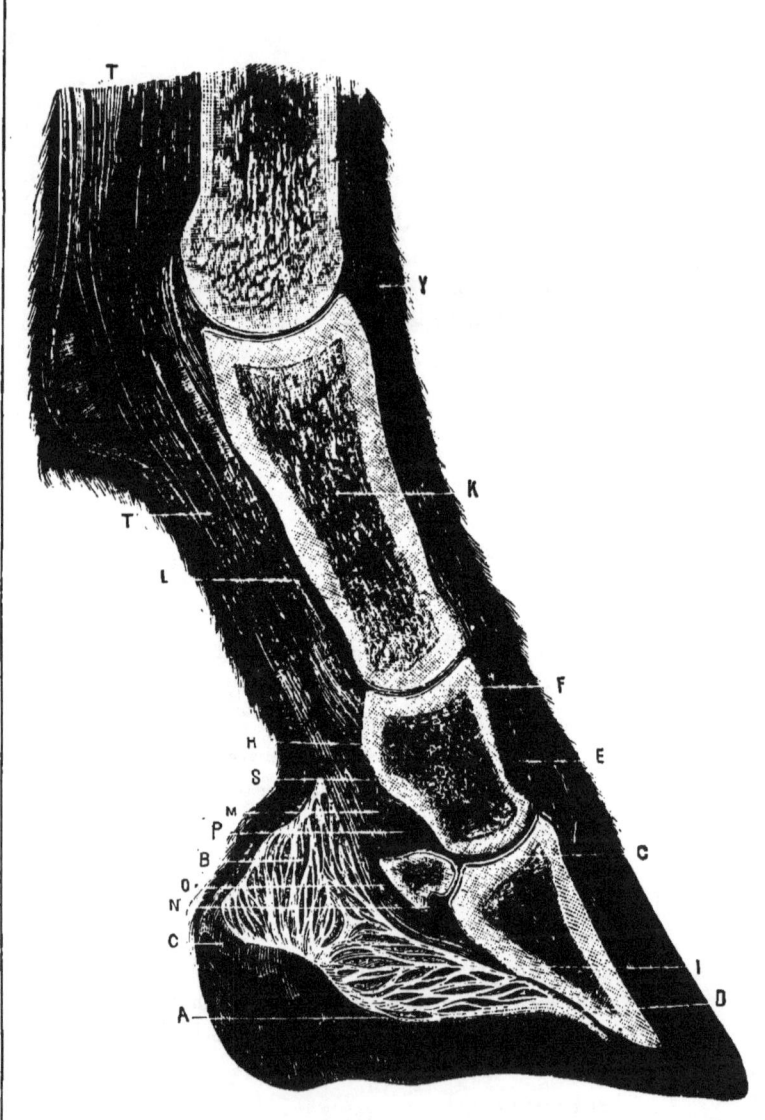

PLATE VII.

PLATE VII.

This plate shows a longitudinal section of the digital region in its median plane.

Its object is to show the spongeous substance in the interior of the bone, the fibrous intersections in the plantar cushion of the articular and tendinous synovial sheaths, and of the plantar cushion (or pad) in the interior of the hoof under the third phalanx and the navicular bone.

- A. Inferior part of the pad (cushion)
- B. Ligamentous bands (filaments) representing the structure of the fibrous body forming the plantar pad.
- C. Enveloping fibrous membrane of the plantar pad.
- D. Point of insertion of the plantar pad to the inferior face of the bone of the foot.
- E. Spongeous substance of the interior of the second phalanx.
- F. Articulation of the first phalanx with the second.
- H. Branches of the perforatus at its insertion to the lateral parts of the second phalanx, or small pastern bone.
- I. Insertion of the plantar aponeurosis to the semi-lunar crest.
- K. Interior of the first phalanx.
- L. Section of the perforatus tendon.
- M. Transverse ligament of the yellow fibrous tissue uniting the anterior face of the perforans to the posterior face of the os coronae, etc. (2d phalanx).
- N. Diverticulum of the sheath of the articulation of the foot between the little sesamoid and the third phalanx.
- O. Little sesamoidal sheath.
- P. Capsule of the articulation of the foot set superiorly against the *cul du sac* of the great sesamoidal sheath.
- T. Perforans tendon.
- Y. Metacarpo-phalangial articulation, or fetlock joint.

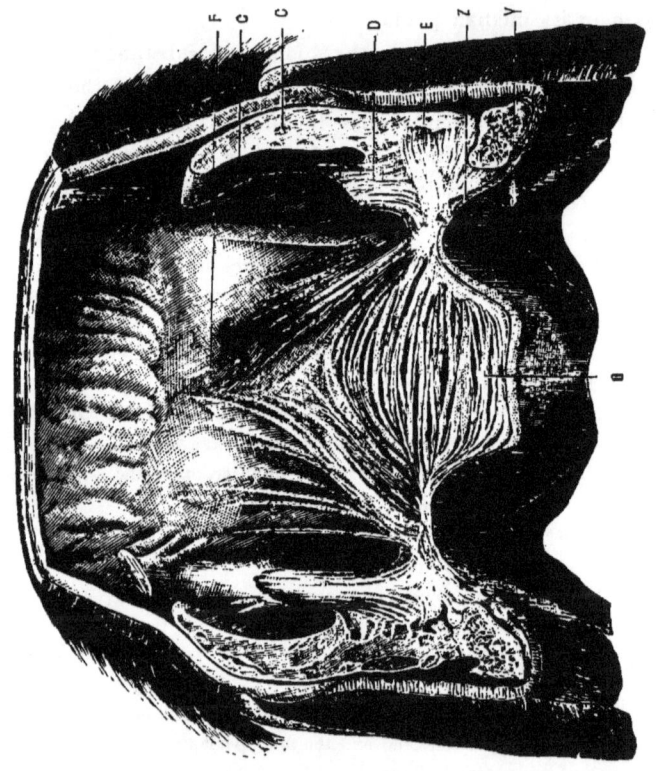

PLATE VIII.

PLATE VIII.

This plate represents a transverse section of the posterior part of the foot behind the phlanges, between the two fibro-cartilages.

It shows the disposition of the bulbs of the plantar pad, or cushion, the stratified layers of the pyramidal body, the hight of the cartilages of the hoof, and the direction of the bars.

- B. Bulb of the plantar pad (or cushion).
- C. Internal face of the fibro-cartilages, or lateral cartilages.
- C'. Hight of the hoof.
- D. Part of the lateral band of the reinforcing sheath of the perforans.
- E. Point of junction of the inferior border of the cartilages with the substance of the plantar pad, or cushion.
- F. Longitudinal depression of the anterior face of the plantar pad.
- G. Stratified layers of the plantar pad in the pyramidal body.
- Z. Superior surface of the bars.
- Y. Thickness and direction of the bars.

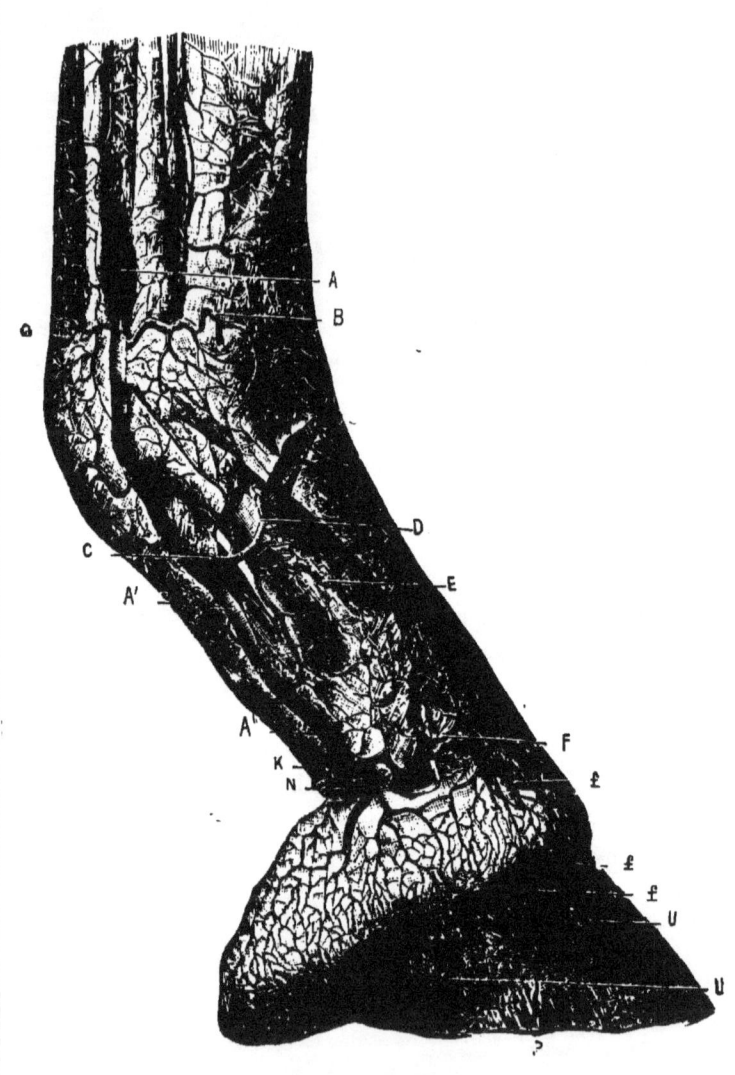

PLATE IX.

PLATE IX.

Arterial Vessels.

The figure shows the superficial disposition of the digital artery on the lateral face of the phalanges.

- A, A', A". Digital artery from its emerging point above the great sesamoids to the point where it disappears under the plate of cartilages in N.
- B. Anterior transverse branch at the metacarpo-phalangial articulation.
- C. Perpendicular artery.
- D. Ascending branch of the perpendicular artery.
- E. Descending branch of the perpendicular artery.
- F. Transverse branch forming with the corresponding one the superficial coronary circle.
- f. Descending ramuscules in the pad of the superficial coronary circle.
- f'. Ascending ramuscules of the podophyllous tissue, or sensitive laminæ.
- G. Posterior transverse branches of the metacarpo-phalangial articulation.
- K. Artery of the plantar pad, or cushion.
- P. Circumflex artery.
- U, U. Ascending terminal divisions of the digital artery; they emerge from the porosities of the third phalanx, and send ramifications to the podophyllous tissue.

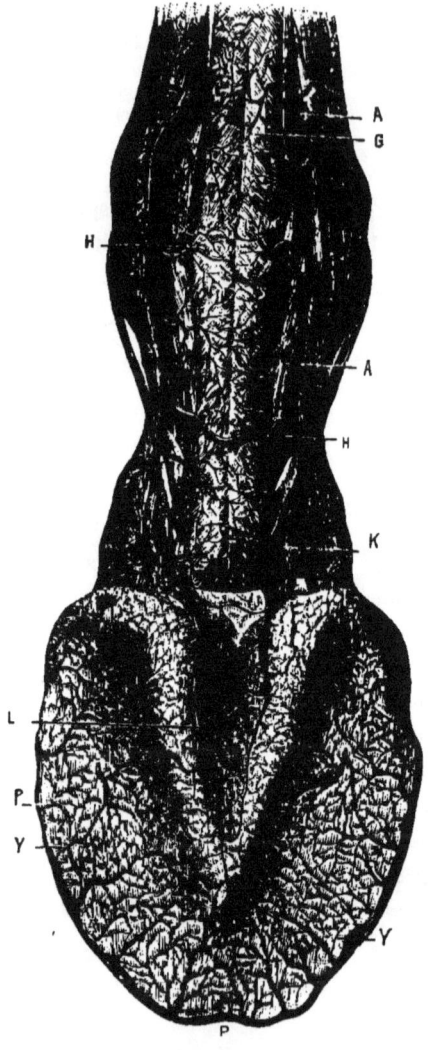

PLATE X.

PLATE X.

Arterial Vessels.

The figure represents the superficial disposition of the digital artery at the superior face of the first two phalanges and at the inferior face of the third.

    A, A'. Digital artery in its passage along the phalanges.
    G. Posterior transverse branches of the metacarpo-phalangial articulation.
    H. Branches above one another at intervals.
    K. Artery of the plantar pad, or cushion.
    L. Internal branch of the artery of the plantar pad.
    P, P, P. Circumflex artery.
    Y, Y. Solar arteries, or arteries of plantar surface.

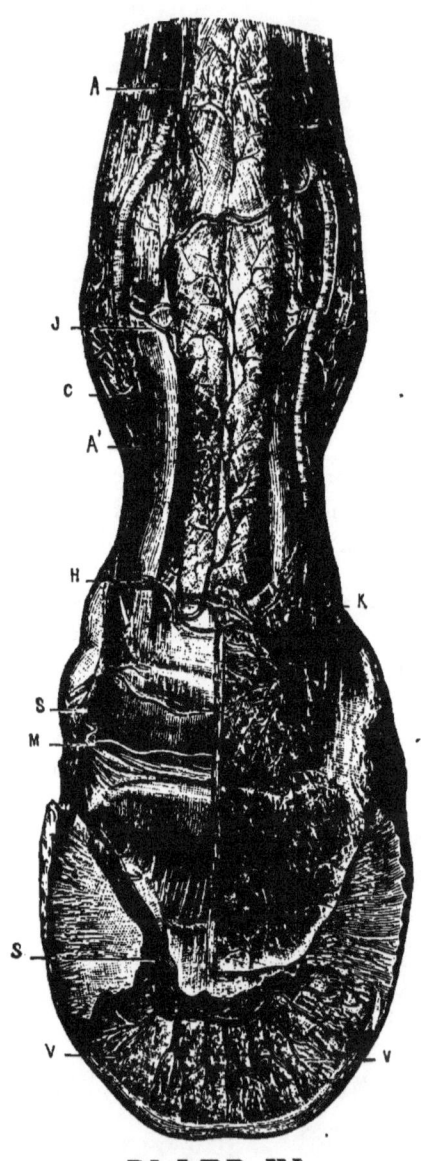

PLATE XI.

PLATE XI.

Arterial Vessels.

The figure shows the deep disposition of the digital artery at the posterior face of the first two phalanges, and in the interior of the third seen from its inferior face.

A, A'. Digital artery.

C. Perpendicular artery at its point of origin.

H. One of the branches running posteriorly, destined to the perforans tendon, in which it ramifies itself.

J. Deep-seated branch.

K. Point of origin of the artery of the plantar pad.

M. Deep transverse branch, completing behind the front superficial coronary circle.

S. *Plantar* artery or posterior terminal branch, in the plantar fissure, and in the semi-lunar sinus, where it forms with its analogue the *semi-lunar* anastomosis.

V, V. *Radiated* divisions of the digital artery emanating from the convexity of the semi-lunar anastomosis, and following the direction of the descending canals of the third phalanx to go and contribute to the formation of the circumflex artery at the exterior circumference of the notched border of the bone.

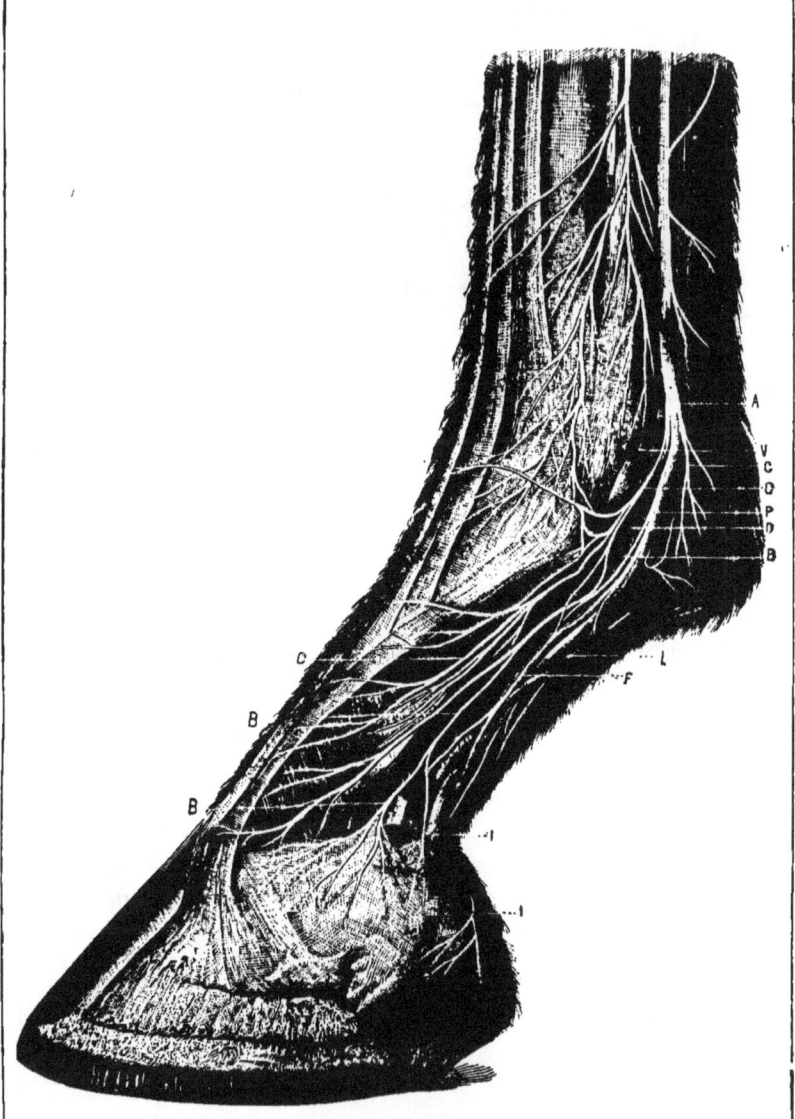

PLATE XII.

PLATE XII.

This figure represents the principle nerves of the digital region.

The plantar nerve occupies the same situation, but the divisions which emanate from it are more numerous and more anastomotic.

P. Plantar nerve.
A. Point of emergence of the plantar nerve above the sesamoids.
B, B. Cartilaginous branch.
C, C. Cutaneous branch.
D. Digital artery.
F'. Bulbous branch.
G. Transverse branch behind the metacarpo-phalangial articulation.
I. Nerve of the plantar pad.
L. Lateral band, or filamentous stay, of the proper tunic of the plantar pad. It crosses obliquely from backward forward, and from upward downward, the direction of the plantar nerve.
V. Digital vein.

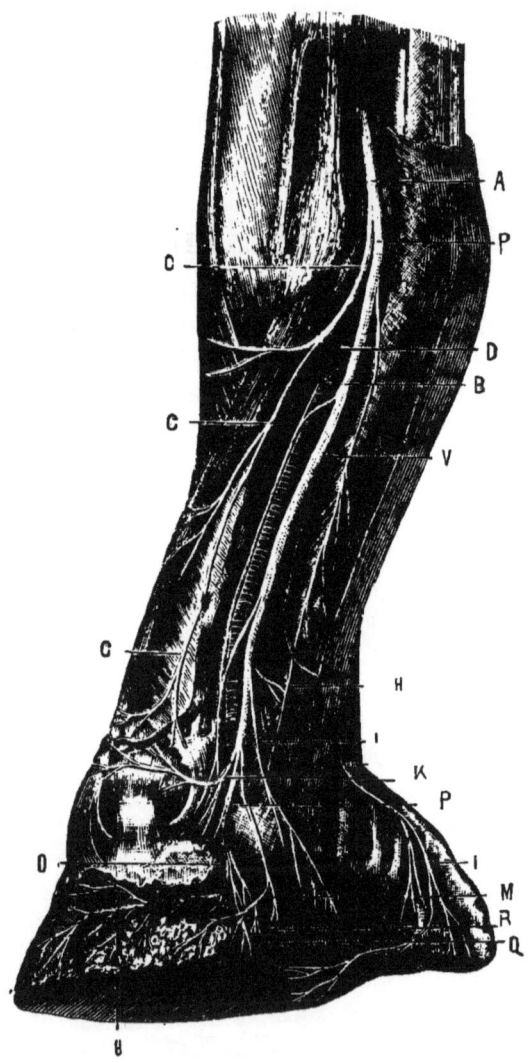

PLATE XIII.

PLATE XIII.

This figure represents on the digital region, seen from three-fourths behind, the disposition of the plantar nerve on the posterior face of the phalanges of the terminal divisions in the interior of the bone of the foot.

- P. Plantar nerve.
- A. Point of emergence of the plantar nerve above the sesamoids.
- B. Cartilaginous branch.
- C. Cutaneous branch.
- D. Digital artery.
- H. Occasional divison destined to the cartilaginous bulbs.
- I, I. Branch of the plantar pad.
- K. Transverse coronary branch.
- M. Podophyllous division.
- O. Pre-plantar nerve.
- Q. Descending branch in the patilobe fissure.
- R. Arterial ramuscules accompanying the digital artery in the plantar fissure.
- V. Vein following sometimes behind the plantar nerve in all its phalangial course. This vessel does not always exist.

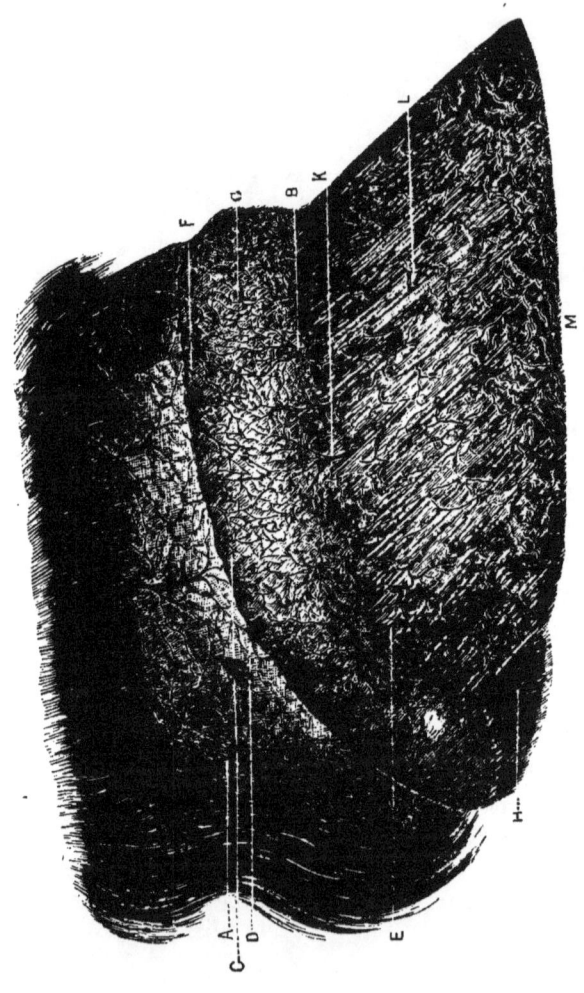

PLATE XIV.

PLATE XIV.

The object of this figure is to show the disposition of the capillary vessels in the tegument of the digital region seen sidewise.

    A, A. Arterial vessels of the skin.

    B, B'. Arterial vessels of the coronary band, or cushion.

    R. Villosities of the coronary cushion. This vessel does not always exist.

This figure represents the principal perioplic bourrelet, the coronary groove and the podophyllous tissue or sensitive laminæ.

    A, B. Principal coronæ (or cutidura) with the villosities covering it.

    C. Superior border of the coronary cushion.

    D. Perioplic coronary groove.

    B. Perioplic (pad) covered with little horny substance.

    F. Inferior border of the cushion.

    G. Podophyllous tissue, or sensitive laminæ.

    H. Villosities of the inferior extremity of the podophyllous laminæ.

    E. Arterial vessels.

    K. Small arterial branches.

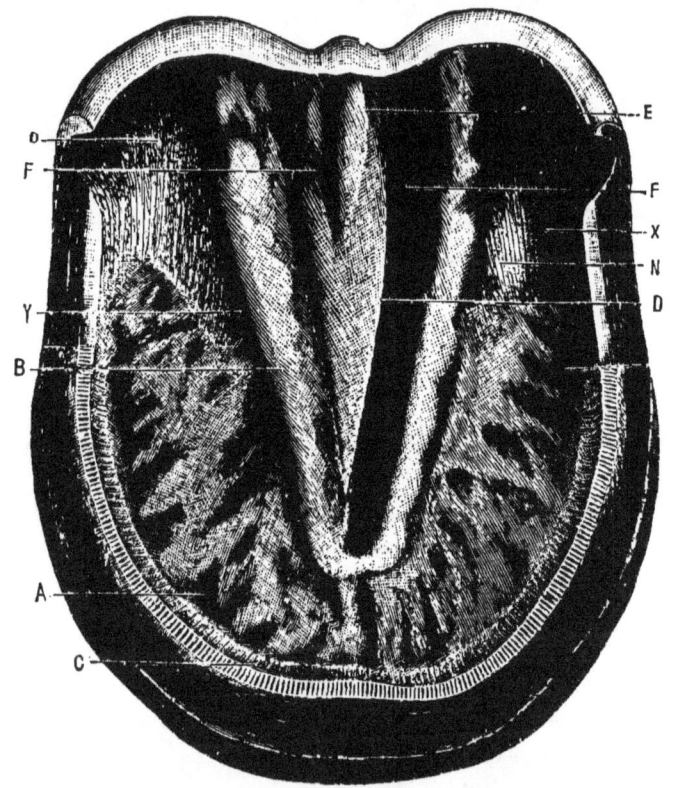

PLATE XV.

PLATE XV.

This figure represents the superior face of the floor of the hoof, formed by the sole and the frog. The wall has been cut at the level of the sole, in order to show the termination of the horny leaves in the edge, or border of the sole

    A. Circular digital cavity at the point of reunion of the sole and the wall.
    B. Superior border of the frog.
    C. Termination of the horny leaves in the edge of the sole.
    D. Cavity formed by the superior face of the frog.
    E. Ridge of the frog, or frog stay.
    F. Groove of the superior face of the frog.
    G. External face of the glomes of the frog.
    N. Keraphyllous tissue at the internal face of the bars.
    O. Cutigeral cavity at the level of the angles of inflection.
    X. Bottom of the angle of inflection.
    Y. Point of termination of the bars at the lateral parts of the frog.

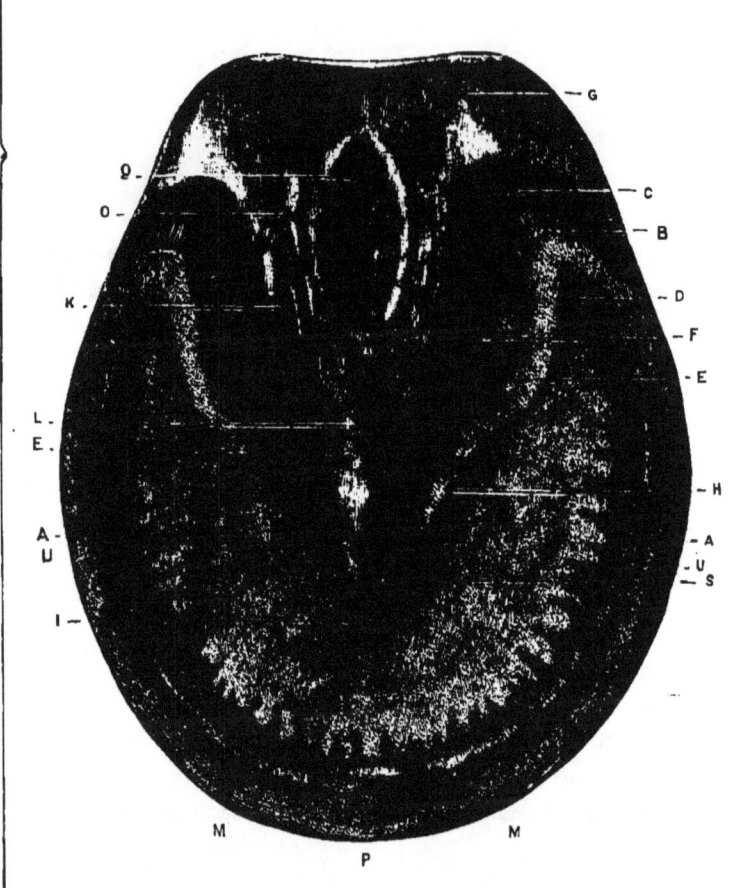

PLATE XVI.

PLATE XVI.

View of the hoof from its inferior face.

P. The wall.
S. The sole.
L. The frog.
A. Line indicating the commissure of the sole and the wall, known as the linea alba, or white line.
B. Angle of inflection of wall of the heels (buttress).
C. Superior border of buttress.
D. Region of the heels of the foot within the angle known as seat of corn.
E. Inferior border of the bars,
F. External face of the bars lining the lateral lacunæ of the frog.
G. Glomes of the frog, or bulbs of the heels.
H. Terminal extremity of the bars at the sides of the frog
I. Point of the frog.
K. Branches of the frog.
M. Regions of the *mamellas* of the hoof.
P. Region of the toe of the hoof.
Q. Median lacuna of the frog.
U. Region of the quarters.

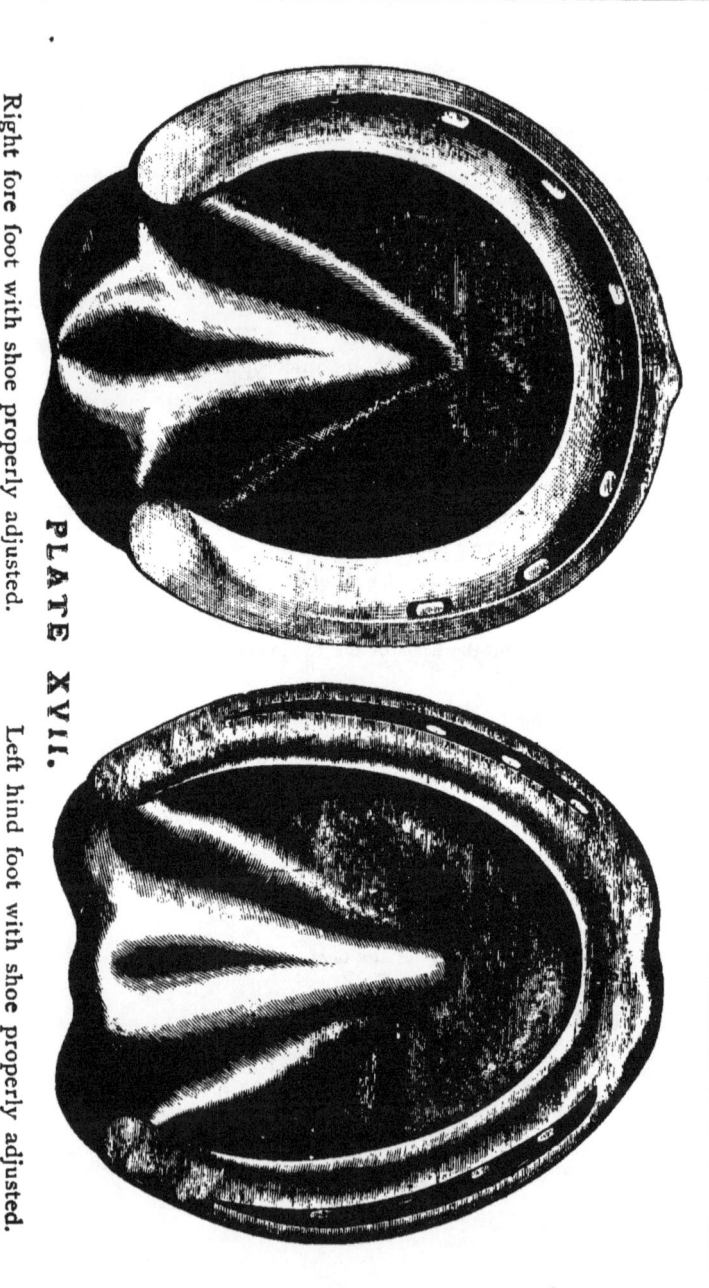

PLATE XVII.

Right fore foot with shoe properly adjusted.

Left hind foot with shoe properly adjusted.

GENERAL INDEX.

PART FIRST.

Abnormal presentations, 611.
Acidity of stomach, 534.
Acute indigestion, 535.
Adams, Dr., on bots, 516.
Adaptation in domestic animals, 28.
Adhesive plaster, a good, 572.
Age, how to tell, 313.
Amaurosis, 586.
Anasarca, 589.
Anchylosis of bones, 411.
Arab horses, docility of, 27.
Arnd horse, 242.
Ascaris, 509.
Ascaris mystax, 511.
Ascites, 587.
Attention in care of horse, 408.
Azoturia, 524.

Back, teaching to, 93, 119.
Back tendons, sprain of, 549.
Bad to bridle, 181.
Bad to shoe, 209.
    Confirmed in the habit, 215.
    Instances of, 213.
    Will not stand, 201
Balking, 193.
    Double, 202.
    Illustrations of, 206.
    Medicine, 196.
    Regular treatment, 198.
    Restless, 199.
    Best treatment, 205.
    Starting the balker, 196.
Balls, giving, 621.
Bellows Falls horse, 220.
Belly, dropsy of, 587.
Biting while grooming, 181.
Bit, "W," or breaking, 88.
    Four-ring, 94, 175.
    Half-moon, 97.
    Spoon, 98.
Bitting, 111.
Bitting rig in training mouth, 110.
Bleeding, 626.
Blind Billy, 275.
Blinders, 255.
    A cause of injury, 256.
    When to use, 123.
    Representative cases, 258.
Blistering for spavin, 419.
Blisters, 613.

Blood, circulation of, 401.
Bloody urine, 519.
Bog spavins, 428.
Bone, anchylosis of, 411.
    Caries of, 412.
    Necrosis of, 413.
Bones of the feet, 331.
Bonner, Robert, eulogy on, 330.
Bony enlargement, 414.
Bots, 513.
Bowels, inflammation of, 502.
Breaking a horse to lead, 101.
    Halter-pullers, 101.
Breaking bit, 88, 191.
Breaking down, 554.
    In breaking balkers, 105.
Breeding, 296.
    Care of the mare, 298.
Bridle, war, 81, 107.
    First form, 81.
    Details of its application, 82.
    Second form, 84.
    Double draw hitch form, 85.
    Secret of using, 87.
Bridle, patent, 99, 189, 206, 225.
Broken knees, 562.
Broken wind, 466.
Bronchitis, 478, 492.
Bronchocele, 471.
Brookville horse, 150.
Bruises, 548.
Bruise of the sole, 540.
    Of the cheeks, 575.
Burrs, use of, 254.

Calks, 540.
    Serious case of, 542.
Canker, 547.
Capped hock, 430.
Care of mare in breeding, 298.
    In going round a horse, 239.
Carelessness in shoeing, results of, 536.
Caries of bone, 412.
    Of tooth, 322.
Carrots, a good laxative, 308.
Cast in stall, 272.
Castration, 608.
Cataract, 586.
Catarrh, 453.
Cathartics, 625.
Catarrhal fever, 473.

(1117)

Causes of injury, 382.
Caustics, 630.
Character spoiled by rough treatment, 234.
Check, overdraw, 173.
Checking and blinders, 246.
 Cruelty of, 246.
 Illustrative cases, 252.
Cheeks, cuts or bruises on, 575.
Chronic cough, 464.
 Founder, 449.
 Rheumatism, 630.
Circulation of blood, 401.
Cleveland horse, 149.
Clicking, 379.
Clinching down nails, 347.
Colic, 493.
 Spasmodic, 495.
 Flatulent, 498.
Collar galls, 605.
Colt, hitching the, 128.
Colt training, 106.
Congestion of lungs, 476, 480.
Constipation, 508.
Contraction, its cure, 351.
Cooking food, 309.
Cord used for war bridle, 82.
Corns, 369.
Cough, chronic, 464.
Counter-irritants, 613.
Cow, to lead a, easily, 274.
Cracked heels, 597, 599.
Crack, quarter, 365.
Crescent shoes, 390.
Cribbing, how to break the habit, 266.
 Gross's device for, 267.
 Throat-strap for same. 267.
 French method of, 269.
Cropping and docking, 247.
Curb, 427.
Cuts or wounds, 568.
Cuts on cheeks, 575.
Cystitis, 518.

Dexter, routine of care of, 310.
Diabetes, 517.
Diaphragm, spasmodic action of, 531.
Diarrhea, 506.
Dick Christian, secret of, 43.
Diseases and their treatment, 401.
Diseases of the bones, 411.
 Eye, 579.
 Feet, 536.
 Lungs, 476.
 Nervous system, 520.
 Skin, 592.
Dislocation of patella, 566.
Diureals, 517.
Division of the tendons, 606.
Docking, 247.
Double balking, 202.
Driving in harness, 118.
 Without reins, 285.
Driving nails, methods of, 345.
Dropsy of belly, 587.

Elbow, tumor on, 604.
Embrocations, 628.
English method of driving nails, 345.
Enlargement, bony, 414.
Epizootic, 473.
Equestrianism, 286.
 Beneficial to health, 293.
 Excessive fear, its effects, 130.
Exostosis, 414.
Eye, diseases of, 579.
 Inflammation of, 581.

False ring-bone, 426.
Farcy, 459.
Fear, 130.
 Of rattle of wagon, 135.
 Top carriage, 136.
 Threshing-machine, 138.
 Robe, 139.
 Umbrella or parasol, 141.
 Sound of a gun, 141.
 Objects while riding or driving. 138.
 Hogs and dogs, 142.
 Railroad cars, 142.
 Jumping out of shafts, 136.
 Insanity, 143.
Feeding and watering, 307.
 Effects of overfeeding, 307.
 Mr. Bonner's system of, 310.
Feet, 298.
 Bones of, 330.
 Kind of in good breeders, 298.
Fetlock, sprain of, 555.
Filaria, 510.
Firing, 420.
 Pyro-puncturing process, 423.
First method of subjection, 52.
Fissure in the toe, 369.
Fistula of withers, 575.
Flatulent colic, 498.
Fleming on paring and rasping, 385.
Foaling, 611.
Follow by the whip, 275.
Fomentations, hot, 616.
Food, cooking the, 309.
Foot, the, 536.
 Accidents and injuries of, 536.
 Lameness, 538.
Foot-strap, 101.
Founder, 441.
Foundered horses, shoeing, 381.
Four-ring bit, 175, 188.
Fractures, 565.
Frog-pressure, 352.

Gadfly, 513.
Galls, collar and saddle, 605.
Gallupville horse, 164.
Gamgee, Prof., on quittor, 544.
Getting cast in stall, 272.
Glanders and farcy, 459.
Glass-eye, 586.
Glass, stepping on, 536.
Gross's device for curing cribbing, 267.

GENERAL INDEX: PART FIRST.

Graveling, 539.
Grease 600.
Great Barrington balking case, 206.

Half-moon bit, 97, 186.
Haltering, simple way of, 115.
Halter-pulling, 101, 222.
    Instances of, 224.
Hamill, Prof., on tip shoeing, 335.
Harnessing, kicking while, 179.
Headstrong stallions, treatment for, 235.
Heaves, 466.
Heels, opening the, 360.
    Weak, 374.
Hen lice, 595.
Herman horse, 234.
Herpes, 597.
Hetrick horse, 149.
High checking, 248.
Hind feet, to shoe, 348.
Hip lameness, 559.
Hip strap, 174.
Hitching a colt, 128.
    To wagon, 121.
    To stand without, 231.
Hives, 593.
Hoof-ointment, 600.
Horseback riding, 286.
Horse distemper, 457.
Hot fomentations, 616.
Hydrothorax, 490.

Idiopathic tetanus, 529.
Indiana stallion, 148.
Indigestion, 534.
    Acute, 535.
Inflammation of bowels, 502.
    Bladder, 518.
    Brain, 520.
    Eyes, 581.
    Feet, 536.
    Kidneys, 516.
    Lungs, 483.
    Os pedis, 452.
    Veins, 590.
Influenza, 473.
Injury, special causes of, 382.
Injuries to the tongue, 574.
Insanity, 143.
Interfering, 378.

Jennings, Dr., on caries of teeth, 463.
Jumping out of shafts, 136.
    Over fences, 273.

Kickers in stall, 176.
    Switching, 170.
    Runaway, 124.
Kicking, 148.
    Common causes of, 151.
    Cows, 273.
    Illustrative cases, 148.
    In stall, 271.
    While harnessing, 179.

Kicking-straps, 171.
Kiss, teaching to, 279.
Knees, broken, 562.
Knuckling over, 561.

Ladies riding, 293.
Lameness, navicular-joint, 432, 556.
    Foot, 538.
    Hip, 559.
    Shoulder, 556.
    Stifle-joint, 567.
Laminitis, 441.
    Dr. Meyer's treatment of, 446.
    Dr. Shepard's, 447.
    Dr. Hamill's, 448.
Lampas, 591.
Lancaster horse, 150.
Laryngitis, 455.
Lead, breaking a horse to, 101.
Lead a cow easily, to, 274.
Leaning over, 221.
Leveling feet for shoeing, 339.
Lie down, teaching to, 279.
Liniments, 629.
Lock-jaw, 528.
Lowering vitality, 39.
Lugging, 190.
Lumbricoides, 512.
Lungs, congestion of, 480.
Lymphangitis, 532.

Mad staggers, 520.
Maine man's method with balkers, 197.
Mallenders, 605.
Mammitis, Appendix, 472.
Mange, 593.
Mansfield mare, 149.
Mare, care of in breeding, 298.
Mc Beth, Dr., on spinal meningitis, 525.
Mc Bride, Prof., on check-rein, 254.
Mc Lellan, Prof., on tip shoeing, 337.
Megrims, 522.
Meningitis, spinal, 524.
Metastasis, 520.
Methods of subjection. First, 52.
    Second, 61.
    Third, 71.
"Monday morning leg," 532.
Mouth, training of, 110.
    Controlling, 183.
    Sore, 575.
Mud fever or scratches, 597.
Mule, treatment of, 263.
    For saddle gall, 265.

Nailing, 343.
    Clinching down, 347.
Nails, driving in deep, 536.
Nails, stepping on, 536.
Nasal gleet, 471.
Navicular-joint lameness, 432, 556.
Necrosis of bone, 413.
Neglect of horses when hitched, 261.
Nervous system, diseases of, 520.

Nettle rash, 593.
Norwalk horse, 150.

Objects, fear of, 138.
Objections in stabling, 302.
Ointments, 572.
    Hoof, 600.
Opening the heels, 360.
    Quarters, Roberge's method, 362.
Open joint, 562.
Ophthalmia, 581.
    Specific or periodic, 583.
Osmer on shoeing, 387.
Overdraw check, 173.
Overloading, 207.
Overreaching, 379, 543.
Oxyures, 510.

Painesville horse, 192.
Paralysis, 527.
    Partial, 524.
Parasites, 509.
Paring foot, evils of, 390.
Parturition, 611.
Patella, dislocation of, 566.
Patent bridle, 99, 189, 206, 225.
Pawing in stall, 271.
Peditis, 452.
Penis, injuries and diseases of, 610.
Pennington horse, 235.
Perforans tendon, strain of, 556.
Performing blind horse, 284.
Peritonitis, 533.
Phlebitis, 590.
Phlebotomy, 626.
Phrenitis, 520.
Physical power, resorting to, 38.
Physicking, 623.
Pink-eye, 475.
Plaster, a good adhesive, 572.
Pleurisy, 476, 486.
Pneumonia, 483.
    Typhoid, 491.
Poling a horse, 117.
Poll-evil, 578.
Poultices, 618.
Prairie hay as food, 307.
Prescriptions and recipes, 635.
Presentations, abnormal, 611.
Pricking in shoeing, 349, 536.
Princess, her feet, 329.
Principles of treatment, 32.
Profuse staling, 517.
Putney horse, 149.
Pulling upon one rein, 190.
Pulse, the, 619.
Pyro-puncturing process, 423.

Qualities for management of horse, 49.
Quarter-crack, 365.
Quittor, 543.

Railway cars, fear of, 142.
Recipes and prescriptions, 635.

Ravenna colt, 150.
Reins, driving without, 285.
Retention of urine, 519.
Rheumatism, 630.
    Acute, 632.
    Chronic, 633.
Riding horseback, 286.
Rigs for throwing, 52.
Ring-bone, 425.
    False, 426.
Ring-worm, 596.
    Vesicular, 597.
Roaring, 469.
Robe, fear of, 139.
Roberts horse, 233.
Rolling motion shoe, 364.
Rowels, 628.
Rucking, 349.
Running away, 183.
Running back in stall, 230.

Saddle and collar galls, 605.
Saddle gall in mules, 265.
Sallenders, 604.
Sand-crack, 369.
Scratches, 597, 599.
Secret of Dick Christian, 43.
Seedy toe, 539.
Setons, 627.
Shafts, jumping out of, 136.
Sheath, foulness of, 610.
Shoe, the rolling motion, 364.
Shoeing, 329.
    Foundered horses, 381.
    Hind feet, 348.
    Nailing, 343.
    Pricking and rucking, 349.
    Tips or thin shoes, 334.
    Trimming, 338.
Shoulder galls, 605.
    Lameness, 556.
    Tumor on, 602.
Side-bone, or false ring-bone, 426.
Sinuses, 570.
Skin, diseases of, 592.
    Ointment for, 600.
Skull, injuries to, 520.
Sleepy staggers, 520.
Sole, bruises of, 540.
Sore throat, 455.
Sore mouth, 575.
Spasmodic colic, 495.
Spasmodic action of the diaphragm, 531.
Spavin, 417.
    Bog, 428.
Special causes of injury, 382.
Spinal meningitis, 524.
Splent, or splint, 415.
Spoiled by fright, 132.
Spoon bit, different forms of, 186.
Sprains, bruises, etc., 548.
Sprains of back tendons, 549.
    Of fetlock, 555.
    Of perforans tendon, 556.

Stabling, 301.
Stables, ventilation of, 303.
Staling, profuse, 517.
Staggers, 520.
Stallions, 232.
    Fred Arnd horse, 242.
    Indiana stallion, 148.
    Jet, 239.
    Herman horse, 234.
    Lancaster horse, 150.
    Roberts horse, 233.
    Treatment for headstrong, 235.
Standing without hitching, 231.
Starting the balker, 196.
Stepping on nails, glass, etc., 536.
Stifle, 566.
Stifle-joint lameness, 567.
Stomach, the, 534.
    Acidity of, 534.
Strangles, 457.
Stringhalt, 530.
Strongyli, 510.
Stumbling, 381.
Subjection, first method, 52.
    Natures that will not bear it, 60.
    Instructions for throwing, 55.
    Second method, 61.
    Third method, 71.
Submission, signs of, 75.
Sun-stroke, 523.
Superpurgation, 506.
Surfeit, 592.
Sutures, 571.
Sweeney, 558.
Swelled legs, 589.
Switching kickers, 170.
Synovial membrane, danger of cutting in throwing, 101.

Tape-worm, 510.
Teaching a sullen colt to lead, 126.
    To follow by the whip, 275.
    To lead with the whip, 128.
    To lie down, 279.
    To stop instantly, 92.
    To tell his age, 277.
Teeth, the, 313.
    Telling the age by, 313.
Tender-bitted, 273.
Tendons, back, sprain of, 549.
    Division of, 606.
Tenotomy, 605, 606.
Tent, dressing with, 569.
Teres lumbrici, 509.
Tetanus, 528.
    Idiopathic, 529.
    Traumatic, 529.
Throat-strap to cure cribbing, 267.
Thorough-pin, 428.
Thrombus, 591.
Throwing, rigs for, 52.
    Instructions for, 55.
    Danger in throwing forcibly, 101.
Thrush, 546.
Thumps, 531.

Tips or thin shoes, 334.
Toe, fissure in, 369.
Tommy, the throwing pony, 283.
Tongue, injuries to, 574.
Tracheotomy, 628.
Training with common halter, 107.
    To lead with whip, 128.
    To handle the feet, 108.
    The mouth, 110.
Treads, 540.
Treatment for very vicious horses, 219.
    For very vicious stallions, 237.
    For headstrong stallions, 235.
Tricks, teaching, 275.
Trichocephalus dispar, 510.
Trimming for shoeing, 338.
Trocar and canula, 501.
Tumor on shoulder, 602.
    On point of elbow, 604.
Tympanites, 498.
Typhoid pneumonia, 491.

Umbrella, fear of, 141.
Upper jaw bit, 94.
Urine, bloody, 519.
    Retention of, 519.
Urticaria, 593.

Veins, inflammation of, 590.
Ventilation of stables, 303.
Vertigo, 522.
Vesicular ring-worm, 597.
Very vicious horses, treatment of, 219, 235, 237.

War bridle, 81.
    Details of its application, 82.
    Double draw hitch form, 85.
    In colt training, 107, 118.
    In treatment of kickers, 176.
    Secret of using, 87.
    With breaking rig, 105.
Watering, 311.
Water in the chest, 490.
Weak heels, 374.
Weed, 532.
Whip, kind of to use, 229.
Wild Pete, 144.
Will not back, 190.
Will not stand, 201.
Wind-broken, 466.
Wind-sucking, 269.
Wind-galls, 430.
Withers, fistula of, 575.
" W," or breaking-bit, 88.
    Point of its use, 92.
Worms, 509.
    Symptoms of, 510.
Wounds, 568.
    Incised, 569.
    Punctured, 571.

Yard, foulness of, 610.
Youatt on colic, 497.

PART SECOND.

Abdominal hernia, 789.
Abortion in cattle, 836.
  In sheep, 929.
Abscess of lungs, 763.
  In swine, 968.
  Section of, 763.
Acute dysentery, 785.
Aerator, milk, 693.
After-pains in ewes, 929.
Afghan fat-tailed sheep, 868, 873.
African beef-eater, 1108.
After-birth retained, 824.
Albuminuria, 795.
Albuminoids in food, 656.
Alsace nose-ring, applied, 851.
American procris, 1104.
Anæmia in cattle, 741.
  In sheep, 899.
  In swine, 969.
Angina, 939.
Anthrax in cattle, 732, 734.
  In sheep, 906.
  In swine, 936, 938.
Ant-thrush, short-tailed, 1112.
Aphtha, epizootic, 737.
Apiary of A. I. Root, 1067.
  Cogswell, 1068.
  Rice, 1070.
  Phelps, 1071.
Apoplexy in cattle, 801.
  In swine, 961.
  Splenic, 736.
  Parturient, 832.
Apple-tree borer, 1097.
Apple-trees, insects injurious to, 1096.
Approach-grafting, 1094.
Argali, 878, 879.
Arteries of stomach, 771.
Ascaris mystax, 1060.
Ascites, 899.
Aseels, 997.
Asthenic hæmaturia, 746.
Asthma, 766.
Aubrace sheep, 876, 878.
Augeron hog, 966.
Auscultation, 752.
Ayrshire bull, 649.
  Heifer, 688.

Bacteridien, 732.
Bandage, many-tailed, 859.
Bandaging udder, 740.
Bark-louse, 1103.
Barns, dairy, 673.
Barrel churn, horizontal, 701.
Bee-culture, 1065.
Bees, physiology of, 1070.
  Three orders of, 1066.
  Formation of eggs, 1071.
  Pasturage, 1077.
  Preparing for winter, 1082.
  Hives, 1080.

Beecher, Rev. H. W., eloquent sermon in behalf of birds, 1109.
Beef-eater, African, 1108.
Beetle, flea, 1104.
  Rose, 1104.
Bird-louse, 1063.
Birds, a plea for the, 1107.
Black tongue, 734.
Blain, 734.
Blanchard churn, 701.
Bladder, inflammation of, 897.
  Protrusion of, 800.
  Stone in, 897.
Blood, diseases of, 899.
Bloodhound, 1047.
Blood-striking, 906.
Blood-sucker, 1063.
Bloody murrain, 732.
Bloody round-worm, 1059.
Bloody urine in cattle, 796.
  In sheep, 901.
Blue-bottle fly, 902.
Blue disease, 945.
Bodkin-tailed round-worm, 1059.
Bordered round-worm, 1058.
Bowels, inflammation of, 1055.
Brahma fowls, 990.
Braxy water, 901.
Breeders in sheep, selection of, 886.
Bronchitis in cattle, 759.
  Verminous, 812.
  In sheep, 894.
  In poultry, 1020.
Budding fruit, 1090.
Buffalo, cross with American cattle, 660.
Bullard's oscillating churn, 701.
Bull-dog, 1045.
"Bull-dogs" applied to nose, 776.
Bumble-foot, 1021.
Butter-making, 686.
  Jars, 705.
  Marketing, 704.
  Working, 701.
  Salting, 703.
  Workers, 703.

Cachexia, 899.
Calculus, 897.
Calf-louse, 812.
Calves, raising, 662.
  Feeding, 666.
  Treatment of, 841.
Calving, 662.
  Time of, 664.
  Treatment in, 664.
Cancerous ulcers, 748.
Canker of foot, 931.
Canker worms in fruit, 1100.
Canula, application of, 765.
Caponizing fowls, 1029.
Caseine in relation to butter, 654.
  Precipitation of, 681.

Cashmere goat, 869, 874.
Castration, 930.
Catarrh, in cattle, 753.
  In sheep, 893.
  In swine, 954, 961.
  In poultry, 1021.
Catheter, 794.
Cattle, breeds of, 648.
  Diseases of, 721.
Cat-flea, 1063.
Charblais bull, 684.
  Cow, 687.
Charbon, in cattle, 732
  In sheep, 906.
  In swine, 936.
Charbonous fever, 732.
Cholera, 1022.
  So-called, 944.
Cheese-making, 706.
  Presses, 713.
  Hoops, 714.
  Factories, 715.
Chester white pig, 958.
Chicken-coops, 1005.
Chiff-chaff, 1107.
Chigger, 1063.
Chinese hog, 941.
Chlorine gas, apparatus for generating, 861.
  For preparing, 862.
Choking, 778.
Chronic dyspepsia, 783.
Churning, 697.
Churns, 698, 699, 700, 701.
Clamp, wooden, 789.
  Iron, 789.
Cleanliness, 859.
Cleft-grafting, 1094.
Clover, 668.
Cochin fowls, 989.
Codling-moths, 1101.
Cœnurus of sheep, 916, 917.
  Cerebralis, 900.
Colds and cough, 962.
Colic, 841.
Constipation, in sheep, 895.
  In swine, 962.
  In dogs, 1055.
Consumption in cattle, 748.
  In poultry, 1022.
Contagious enteric fever, 729.
Cooley's creamer, 695.
Cotswold sheep, 876, 877.
Cotyledons, 824.
Cough and colds, 962.
Cow, points of, 643.
Cows, treatment of during gestation period, 664.
Cow-pox, 739.
Cramps, 1022.
Cream, raising of, 686.
  Apparatus, 695.
Cretan, or Wallachian sheep, 871, 874.
Crevecœurs, 987.
Crop-bound, 1023.
Croup, 841.
Curculio, plum, 1103.

Curd breakers, 710.
  Drainer, 709.
  Mill, 710.
Currant-worm, 1105.
Cysticercus bovis, 814.
  Cellulosus, 976.
Cystitis, 799.

Dachshund, 1052.
Dairy barn, model, 673.
Dairy interest, importance of, 643.
  Barns, 673.
Dangerous cattle, device for controlling, 852.
Danish dog, 1045.
Danubian goose, 998.
Debility, 1023.
Delivery milk-cans, 716.
Delwart's truss, 827.
Dermanyssus avium, 1064.
Dermatocoptes, 812.
Devon cattle, 650.
Diabetes, 793.
Diarrhea in cattle, 784.
  In calves, 842.
  In sheep, 895.
  In swine, 963.
  In poultry, 1023.
  In dogs, 1054.
Dingo, 1033.
Diseases of cattle, 721.
  Of sheep, 891.
  Of swine, 933.
  Of poultry, 1020.
  Of dogs, 1053.
Dishley sheep, 866, 872.
Diphtheria in swine, 964.
  In poultry, 1024.
Dipping sheep, 886.
Disinfection, 859.
Distemper, 1054.
Distention of rumen, 895.
Docking, 931.
Dogs, races of, 1031.
  Diseases of, 1053.
Dog-fighting, 1045.
Dog-flea, 1063.
Dog-tick, 923.
Dorsetshire pig, 952.
Drainage, 671.
Drenching a cow, 768.
Dropping the cud, 782.
Dropsy, 899.
Ducks, 998.
  Worms in, 1029.
Durham cow, short-horn, 733.
Dysentery in cattle, 785.
  In sheep, 895.
  In dogs, 1054.
Dyspepsia, 782.

Ear-louse, dog, 1063.
Echinococcus, 1061.
Echinorrynchus Polymorphus, 1029.
Ecthyma, 905, 906.
Ectozoa, 808.

GENERAL INDEX: PART SECOND.

Eczema, in cattle, 804.
  In sheep, 900.
Egg-bound, 1024.
Eggs, physiology of, 1008.
  Incubation, 1009.
  Packing and preserving, 1001.
  Testing, 1011.
Eggs of bees, 1070.
  Queen's egg under microscope. 1071.
Egg-protectors, 1010.
  Egg-testers, 1011.
Egyptian goose, 998.
Emphysema, 766.
Emprosthotonos, 803.
Enteric fever, 729.
Enteritis, 787.
Entozoa, 812.
Epilepsy, in cattle, 801.
  In swine, 966.
Epizootic aphtha, 737.
  Epizootic catarrh in swine, 954.
Escutcheon, milk, 646.
Esquimau dog, 1043.
Essex boar, 950.
  Pig, 951.
Examination of pulse in ox, 724.
Exmoor sheep, 877, 879.
Extravasation, bloody, in papillæ of skin, 729.

Fairlamb can, 694.
Fardel-bound, 780.
Feather-eating, 1024.
Feeding, artificial, 656.
Feeling the pulse, 932.
Fetus of cow, 817, 818, 819.
Fezzan sheep, 879, 880.
Filaria imitis, 1062.
  Strongylus, 915.
Flanders bull, 669.
  Cow, 677.
Flat-headed apple-tree borer, 1097.
Flea-beetle, 1104.
Flies, 808, 810, 811, 910, 911, 925, 926.
Flooding, 825.
Fluke, 913.
Fluke disease, 913.
Fodder or hay louse, 923.
Food, conditions of giving to cattle, 652.
  Regulation of, 657.
Foods of various kinds, table of, 656.
  Nutritive foods for sheep, table of, 889.
Foot and mouth disease in cattle, 737.
  In sheep, 904.
  Foot-rot, or foot-halt, 902.
Foot-louse, 926.
Foul in cattle, 805.
  In sheep, 902.
Fowls, breeds of, 983.
Fragility of bones, 783.
French boar, 960, 963.
  Sow, 962, 965.
French ox-harness, 853.
Frizzled fowls, 991.
Frost-bite, 1025.
Fruit culture, 1087.

Gad-fly, 808, 810, 811, 910, 911.
Gags, wooden, 773.
  Iron, 774.
Gamasus of fodder, 812.
Gang cheese-press, 711.
Gangrenous angina, 939.
Gapes, 1025.
Garget, 930.
Geese, 998.
Giant strongle, 1059.
Gid, 916.
Giddiness, 1025.
Glos anthrax in cattle, 734.
  In swine, 938.
Glossina morsitans, 925.
Glossitis, 769.
Goitre, 1056.
Gonorrhea in cattle, 839.
  In sheep, 897.
Goat, Cashmere, 869, 874.
Gout, 1025.
Grafting, 1093.
Grape-vine bark-louse, 1103.
  Flea-beetle, 1104.
Grass, best food for cow, 657.
  When to cut, 668.
Greyhound, 1046.
  Persian, 1046.
Gullet, obstruction of, 778.
  Sacular dilatation of, 780.
Gut-tie, 791.

Hæmatopinus vituli, 812.
  Eurysternus, 812.
Hæmaturia, 746.
Hæmorrhagica, pupura, 742.
Hair-worms, 921.
Hampshire-downs sheep, 875, 877.
Hay-loader, 671, 672.
  At work, 673.
Hay-making, 668.
Hay-maker, 670, 671.
Heart infested with measles, 814.
Hereford cattle, 650.
Hernia, abdominal, 789.
  Umbilical, 789.
  Of uterus, 838.
Herpes, 804, 805.
Highland sheep, 869, 874.
Hippoboscus ovis, 924.
Holland bull, 717.
  Cow, 727.
Hollow-horn, or horn-ail, 742.
Holstein vertical churn, 697.
Honey extractor, 1079.
Honey, liquid and comb, 1078.
  Storing and marketing, 1083.
  To prevent candying, 1084.
Hooking, device to prevent, 852.
Hoose, 812.
Hoove, 895.
Horn-ail, 742.
Horse-rake, 671, 672.
Houdan fowls, 986.
House-fly, 912.

GENERAL INDEX: PART SECOND.

Hoven in cattle, 770.
  In sheep, 895.
Human remedies, Appendix, 1115.
Human body-louse, 923.
  Head-louse, 924.
Hunting-dog, 1034.
Husk, 812.
Hyena, brown, 1032.
Hybrid bees, how to tell from pure Italians, 1076.
Hydatids, 916, 917, 918.
  In brain of sheep, 917.
Hydrophobia in sheep, 908.
  In dogs, 1057.
Hypoderm, 1063.
Hysterocele, 837, 838.

Ibex, 864.
Ictero-verminous cachexia, 902.
Impacted rumen, 774.
Impaction of omasum, 780.
Imported currant-worm, 1105.
Incubation, natural process of, 1009.
  Artificial, 1012.
Incubators, the Graves, 1013.
  The Halsted, 1014.
  The Boyle, 1015.
  The Tomlinson, 1016.
  The thermostatic, 1017.
  Hearson's regulator, 1018.
Indigestion in lambs, 896.
  In fowls, 1026.
Inflammation of the bladder in cattle, 799.
  In sheep, 897.
  Of the bowels, 1055.
  Of the brain, 801.
  Of the kidneys, 798.
  Of the lungs, 967.
  Of the mouth, 769.
  Of the tongue, 769.
  Of the udder, 839.
  Of the uterus, 828.
Influenza, 901.
Interdigital canal, 903.
Intestines, tape-worm in, 919.
Inversion of the bladder, 800.
  Of the uterus, 825.
Insects, organs of respiration of, 921.
  Injurious to fruit, 1096.
Insolation, 901.
Intestines of ox, 770.
Irritation of vagina, 929.
Itch, 972.

Jersey short-horn cow, 651.

Kidneys of ox, 792.
Koumiss, 719.

Lamb-creep, 885.
Lambing, 927.
Lambs, extra feeding of, 885.
  Management of, 884.

Laryngitis, 756.
Layering, 1093.
  By elevation, 1093.
Leicester sheep, 865, 872.
Lesser pettichaps, 1107.
Left side of cow laid open, 775.
Leg-weakness, 1026.
Leucorrhea, 835.
Lice in cattle, 810.
  In sheep, 923, 924, 925, 926.
  In poultry, 1026.
Light Brahma fowls, 990.
Lincolnshire sheep, 875, 876.
Linguatula serrata, 1062.
Lithiasis, 799.
Liver fluke, 913.
Liver rot in sheep, 913.
Liver disease in poultry, 1027.
Lobule of milk-gland, 679.
  Of mammary gland in woman, 680.
Lock-jaw in cattle, 802.
  In sheep, 899.
Long-horn cattle, 650, 657, 658.
Longford cheese-factory, 714.
Loo, or low, 902.
Lower jaw of cow in rinderpest, 728.
Lucilia homnivorax, 925.
Lungs, abscess of in cattle, 763.
  In swine, 968.
Lymphatic gland, 772.

Maggots, 912.
Milignant gangrenous angina, 939.
  Pustule, 732.
  Sore throat in cattle, 734.
  In swine, 946.
  Epizootic catarrh, 954.
Mammary gland of woman, 680
  Lobules of, 680.
Mammitis, 839.
  Dr. C. A. Meyer, on Appendix, 1114.
Man-eating fly, 925.
Mange in cattle, 810.
  In sheep, 921.
  In swine, 972.
  In dogs, 1064.
Maw-bond, 774.
McBeth, Dr. B. C., on inversion of uterus, 826.
Measles in cattle, 813.
  In swine, 974.
Measly beef, 813.
Meat-fly, 912.
Medicine, how to administer, 723.
Merino sheep, 871, 872, 874.
Metritis, 828.
Metro-peritonitis, 829.
Meyer, Dr. C. A., on mammitis, Appendix, 1114.
  On inversion of uterus, 825.
  On caponizing fowls, 1029.
Milk, composition of, 680.
  Pure conditions of, 682.
  Danger of imparting disease, 683.
  Cooling and setting, 689–692.
  Delivery, 716.
  Milk secretion, 676.

1126 GENERAL INDEX: PART SECOND.

Milk-aerator, 693.
 Cans, 694.
 Strainers, 690.
 Tanks, 690.
 Vats, 706.
Milk-escutcheon of cow, 646, 647, 648.
Milk-fever, 832.
Milk-gland, network of, 678.
 Lobule of, 679.
Milking, 659.
 Hints in regard to, 662.
 Season of, 664.
 Milking machines, 662.
Milking-pails, 661.
Milk-shelves, revolving, 689.
Mirror-escutcheon, 646.
Moufflon sheep, 878, 880.
Mouth, injuries of, 768.
 Inflammation of, 769.
Mowing machines, 670.
Mully cattle, 651.
Murrain, 906.

Nævus, section of, 750.
Nephritis, 798.
Nervous debility in parturition, 802.
Newfoundland dog, 1035.
Nile goose, 996.
Norfolk sheep, 874, 875.
Nose-piece to prevent sucking, 666.
Nose-clamps, 850.
Nose-punch, 851.
Nose-ring, 850.

Obstruction of gullet, 778.
Oestrus bovis, 810.
Omasum, impaction of, 780.
Ophisthotonos, 803.
Ophthalmia, 806.
Oscillating churn, 699.
Ostea sarcoma, 748.
Ox, kidneys of, 792.
 Urinary apparatus of, 792.
 Urethral canal of, 793.
Ox-louse, 812.
Ox's head, 722.
Ox prepared for casting, 790.
 For bleeding, 833.
Ox harness, French, 853.
 Travis, 850.
Ox measle, 814.
Oxyuris vermicularis, 1060.
Oyster-shell bark-louse, 1098.

Pan for setting milk, 689.
Paralysis of hind quarters, 980.
Paraphlegia, parturient, 900.
Parasites, discoveries in, by microscope, 909.
 Their ravages, 1057.
Parasitic diseases of cattle, 808.
 Of sheep, 909.
 Of swine, 970.
 Of poultry, 1025.
 Of dogs, 1057.

Parturient apoplexy, 831, 832.
 Paraplegia, 900.
Parturition, nervous debility in, 902.
Pasturage, 882.
Pair-tree twig-girdler, 1102.
Peccary, 965.
Pekin bantams, 995.
Pendulum churn, 699.
Peregourd hog, 967.
Pentastomum denticulatum, 1062.
 Tenoides, 1062.
Peritonitis, 788.
Pet dogs, 1052.
Pfriemenschwantze, 1060.
Phrenitis, 801.
Phthisis, 748.
Pigmy Piculet, 1110.
Piles, 969.
Pining, 899.
Pip, 1027.
Planarian, 914.
Playfair's, Dr. Lyon, analysis of milk, 654.
Plea for the birds, 1107.
Plethora, 741.
Pleurisy, 763.
Pleuritis, 894.
Pleuro-enteritis, 945.
 Erysipelatous form, 946.
Pleuro-pneumonia, 726.
Pleurostliotonos, 803.
Plexus of lymphatics, section of, 771.
Plum-curculio, 1103.
Plymouth Rock fowls, 989.
Pneumonia in cattle, 761.
 In sheep, 894.
 In swine, 967.
Poland-China pig, 959.
Polish fowls, 990.
Polled cattle, 651.
 Model polled bull, 659.
Portable poultry-houses, 1003.
Potato-cleaner, 980.
Poultry, breeds of, 983.
 Feeding and marketing, 999.
 Architecture, 1003.
 Diseases of, 1020.
Probang and gag, 773.
 Holding cow for passage of, 779.
Protrusion of bladder, 800.
Pruning fruit, 1088.
Psoriasis, in cattle, 804.
 In sheep, 901.
Puerperal fever, 829.
 Paraplegia, 900.
Pulse, feeling the, 932.
Purples, 945
Purpura hæmorrhagica, 742.
Pyæmia, 747.
Pyramidal strainer, 694.

Rabies in sheep, 908.
 In dogs, 1057.
Rectangular churn, Whipple's, 700.
Red mange, 1064.

GENERAL INDEX: PART SECOND.   1127

Red water in cattle, 746.
  In sheep, 901.
Remedies, human, 1115.
Renault's truss, 829.
Rennet, 681.
Retained after-birth, 824.
Retention of urine in cattle, 793.
  In sheep, 897.
Revolving milk shelves, 689.
Revolving barrel churn, 698.
Rheumatism in cattle, 743.
  In sheep, 930.
  In poultry, 1027.
Rickets, 783.
Rinderpest, 729.
Ring-worm, 810, 813.
Romney marsh sheep, 865, 872.
Rose-beetle, 1104.
Rose-colored pastor, 1111.
Rot, 913.
Rot dropsy, 902.
Round-headed apple-tree borer, 1097.
Round-worms, 1059.
Roup, 1027.
Rueff's method of throwing the ox, 849.
Rumen, distention of, 895.
  Impacted, 774.
Rumenotomy, 776.
  Rumen exposed in, 777.
Rumpless bantams, 991.

Sacular dilatation of gullet, 780.
Salting butter, 703.
Scab in sheep, 921, 922.
  In swine, 972.
Scalpel, 758.
Sclerostoma syngamus, 1025.
Scolex of tape-worm, 919, 1061.
Scours in calves, 784.
  In swine, 963.
Sebastopol goose, 998.
Schwartz system of milk cooling, 691.
  Swedish system, 690.
Sediment in urinary canal, 897.
Sebright fowls, 997.
Septicæmia, 747.
Setter, 1051.
  Irish, 1052.
Sharpening mower-knife, 671.
Shearing sheep, 887.
Sheep, breeds of, 863.
  Care and management of, 881.
  Care and feeding in winter, 888.
  Profits of an investment in, 890.
  Selection of breeders, 886.
  Skeleton of, 891.
  Washing and shearing, 887.
Sheep-bug, 925.
Shepherd dog, 1041.
Short-horn cattle, 648, 655.
Short-tailed ant-thrush, 1112
Silky fowls, 990.

Skeleton of cow, 721.
  Of sheep, 891.
  Of hog, 954.
  Of fowl, 1021.
  Of dog, 1053.
Skin-louse, 1064.
Skull of ram, 892.
Small-pox, 905.
Snuffles, 961.
So-called cholera, 944.
Softening of the bones, 783.
Solary erythema, 901.
Sore teats, 838.
Sore throat in cattle, 756.
  Malignant, 734.
Southdown sheep, 867, 872.
Splenic apoplexy, 736.
Sprains, 932.
Staggers, 966.
Stall for two cows, 675.
St. Bernard dog, 1038.
Steinbock, 864.
Sthenic hæmaturia, 797.
Stifle joint, injury of, 855.
Stomach of ruminants, 769, 770.
  Arteries of, 771.
Stomach-pump, 831.
Stone in bladder, 897.
Strangulation of intestines, 791.
Streamlet churn, 699.
Strobile, 919.
Strongle, giant, 1059.
Strongylus or strongula, 979.
Sturdy, 916.
Sucking, methods to prevent, 667.
Suffolk sow, 955.
Sulphuric acid gas, apparatus for liberating, 861.
Sussex cattle, 650.
Suture needles, 857, 859.
Sutures, 857.
Swarming of bees, 1072.
  Prevention of, 1075.
Swelled legs in fowls, 1025.
Swiss bull, 663.
  Cow, 665.
Syrian sheep, 868, 874.
Syringe, glass, 750.
  Hypodermic, 759.
  For wounds, 858.

Tænia, 974.
  Plicata, 919.
  Solium, 974.
  Echinococcus, 1061.
Tamworth pig, 956.
Tank for setting milk, 690.
Tape-worm in cattle, 814.
  In sheep, 919.
  In swine, 974.
  In dogs, 1061.
Teat siphons, various forms of, 739.
Teats, sore, 662.
Tedding machine, 670.

1128 GENERAL INDEX: PART SECOND.

Teeth of cattle, 844.
    Of sheep, 892.
    Of swine, 955.
Terriers, 1051.
Tetanus in cattle, 802.
    In sheep, 899.
Thread-strongle, 915.
Throwing ox, methods of, 849.
Ticks in sheep, 886.
Tongue, inflammation of, 769.
    Paralysis of, 769.
Tonics, 1028.
Traumatic, albuminuria, 795.
Trichina spiralis, 977.
Trichinosis, 976.
Trichocephalus dispar, 1060.
Trichodectes of ox, 812.
Trocar, 774.
Truss for hernia, 789.
    Delwart's, 827.
    Renault's, 829.
Tsetse fly, 926.
Tubercular consumption, 748.
Tuberculosis, 748.
Tumor on parotid glands, and on upper and lower jaw, 749, 750.
    Tumor cured by quack, 749.
Turkeys, 993.
Turnips, pulped, as food, 657.
Turnsick, 916.
Twig-girdler, 1102.
Tympanites, 770.

Udder of cow, 678.
    Of rabbit, 681.
    Bandaging, 740.
    Described, 676.
    Inflammation of, 939.
    Lobule and milk ducts of, 678.
Udders of good milkers, 682.
Ulcers, cancerous, 748.
Umbilical hernia, 789.
Unnatural presentations, 820, 821.
    Halters for operation in, 822.
Uræmia, 745.

Urinary apparatus of ox, 792.
Urine, retention of, 793.
    Incontinence of, 795.
    Operation for removing urine from ox, 746.
Uterus of cow, 824.

Van Beneden on the tape-worm, 919.
Variola vaccinæ, 739.
Ventilation, 859.
Vertical churn, 697, 698.
Vesicles of mammary lobules, 681.
Victoria churn, 698.

Wallachian sheep, 871, 874.
Wallikiki fowls, 994.
Warragal, 1033.
Washing sheep, 887.
Water braxy, 901.
Weighing can, 695.
Weldon's cream-raising apparatus, 695.
Welsh sheep, 877, 879.
Whipple's rectangular churn, 700.
White comb, in fowls, 1028.
Whites, 835.
White scours, 896.
Wild boar of Africa, 934.
    Of India, 935.
    Of Europe, 937.
    Of Malacco, 939.
Willow warblers, 1107.
Wool, comparison of fibers, 874.
Woolly louse of the apple, 1097.
Wounds, incised, 857.
    Lacerated, 858.
    Punctured, 859.
    Contused, 859.
    In swine, 980.
Wren, yellow, 1107.
    Golden-crested, 1108.
    Fire-crested, 1108.

Yellow wren, 1107.
Yokohama fowls, 989.
Yorkshire hog, 945, 946, 947.

APPENDIX

	PAGE.
The Farm	1129–1137
Grasses, Haymaking, etc.	1138–1169
Water and Germs	1170–1181

www.ingramcontent.com/pod-product-compliance
Lightning Source LLC
Chambersburg PA
CBHW031122160426
43192CB00008B/1084